The Family Contract
A BLUEPRINT FOR
SUCCESSFUL PARENTING

by

HOWARD I. LEFTIN, M.D.

T·H·E
PIA
PRESS

DEDICATION

To Mom and Dad

ACKNOWLEDGEMENTS

For their valuable contributions to this book, I would like to thank Ms. Karla Dougherty, Mr. Dan Montopoli and Mr. Larry Chilnick.

For her insightful advice and support, thanks to my practice associate, Ms. Alyson Mare.

For their generous gestures of encouragement, without which this book would not have been possible, thanks to Mr. Dave Polunas and Ms. Holly Butcher at Laurelwood Hospital, and Mr. Pete Alexis and Mr. Norm Zober of Psychiatric Institutes of America.

For keeping the "alligators" off me while I worked on this project, many thanks to my office manager, Ms. Donna Wilkins.

Finally, for just being the beautiful kids they are, my thanks to Heather, Lauren and Larisa.

Cover illustration by Al Gold.

About Arbor Hospital

Arbor Hospital of Greater Indianapolis is the area's newest psychiatric hospital located on 21 acres at 111th Street and North Pennsylvania. As one of 60 psychiatric hospitals in the United States operated by Psychiatric Institutes of America, Arbor Hospital is a unique resource dedicated to meeting the needs of the community. Arbor Hospital provides treatment programs for children, adolescents, and adults which reflect PIA's philosophy for the diagnosis and treatment of mental health disorders tied to a strong academic environment.

The JOURNEY® program, offered to adolescents at Arbor, is a unique program, experiential in nature, that is designed to give adolescents a proactive opportunity for coming to grips with the major emotional demands of their developmental stages of life. The program uses a wide variety of activities including guided imagery, personal inventory exercises, opportunities for self-reflection, and creative problem solving to provide a fun and adventurous opportunity for growth and change.

All patients at Arbor Hospital have an opportunity to participate in art, music, or recreational therapies through an extensive Expressive Therapy program. Through occupational therapy, patients learn specific ways to make use of their free time, and learn to work together to accomplish specific tasks.

Led by the Medical Director, the hospital's multidisciplinary team develops a comprehensive treatment plan for each patient on an individual basis that is geared toward a smooth transition back into the individual's home, work, and/or school life. Individual, group, and family therapy are incorporated into the treatment plan to provide and intense therapeutic environment.

Arbor Hospital also provides individualized, free assessments for persons having mental, emotional or behavioral difficulties. Anyone can speak with a counselor 24-hours a day by calling (317)-575-1000.

The hospital also serves the community by providing community education workshops, prevention and wellness workshops, professional training, and medical education.

The staff at Arbor Hospital brings years of specialized psychiatric experience to the Indianapolis area, and is dedicated to providing our patients with the highest quality of care available.

(317) 575-1000

Table of Contents

About The Author

Dr. Leftin is a psychiatrist certified by the American Board of Psychiatry and Neurology, a member of the American Psychiatric Association and the Houston Psychiatric Society. He obtained his B.A. (magna cum laude, Mathematics) from Boston University in 1973, his M.D. from Baylor College of Medicine in 1977, and completed his four year residency in psychiatry at Baylor in 1981, where he was recipient of the Laughlin Award. Dr. Leftin has been the Medical Director of Laurelwood Hospital in the Woodlands since 1984. He has been practicing general adult and adolescent psychiatry in the North Houston/Woodlands/Conroe area since 1981, treating patients in hospital, day hospital and outpatient settings. (Office:713-367-2187.) Dr. Leftin has extensive experience in treating depression and anxiety-related disorders, as well as adolescent behavioral disorders, alcoholism and drug abuse.

And yes, he has kids.

We, the Parents...

- No sneaking out of the house
- No taking drugs or alcohol
- No lying to parents
- No sexual acting out

No, this isn't a list written by a teenager from an alien world. Nor is it some parent's rich fantasy life. These are rules, straightforward and simple, taken from this book's basic family contract. What's a *family contract*? Briefly, it's a series of rules between parent and child, with corresponding penalties if these rules are broken. Of course, as lawyers are fond of pointing out, even the simplest contract needs to be taken seriously. This book, then, not only provides you with a sample contract, but also explains how it can help you raise healthy, happy, and successful kids.

Terrific. Another book on raising kids that you won't have time to read. Let's face it. The very suggestion that a modern parent can find time even to read the package directions for mushroom soup elicits condescending laughter. But a child who comes home at 2:00 A.M. on school nights, who kicks the sofa every time he gets angry, who spends homework time chattering on the telephone, is no laughing matter.

So what do you do? Turn to those omnipotent "experts" —and their books on raising kids. Unfortunately, their authoritative-sounding advice doesn't always work in the real world of parent and teen.

For those who have heard the opinions of all these "experts" yet still find their kids slowly but inexorably driving them up the proverbial wall, let me reassure you: this is not your typical book written by your typical expert. (As I see it, an "expert" is a guy from out of town with a box of slides. I don't even own a projector.)

So why did I write this book? Because I know (on both a personal and a professional level) the problems difficult kids can cause, and—even more important—I think I can help parents deal with these problems.

So, how did I get to be so presumptuous? Well...

I am a practicing psychiatrist. Yes, I admit it. While it's true that sometimes you can't tell the doctors from the patients without a score card these days, I would remind you that the mental health field has produced such luminaries as Freud, Jung, and Brothers.

The family contract concept is adapted from methods I use at Laurelwood Hospital's program for troubled teenagers. For years I have seen how some of the most difficult teens—the types you would see only on a Mafia recruitment poster—respond to a treatment contract. Hmmm, why not apply the concepts behind this contract to my own family?

When I first introduced the family contract in my own home, my two daughters immediately protested (quite accurately) that I was "bringing the hospital home." I'll never forget, however, that on the same day they complained about the contract, they also washed the car, bathed the dog, did the dishes, and cleaned the bathroom. I'm still recuperating from the emotional shock.

It works.

FAMILY CONTRACT 101

Sometimes therapists get so preoccupied with analyzing problems that they forget to address the main concerns of parents who ask for help with their kids. Of course parents want to understand what's causing the problems at home, but they also want to know what to *do* about them. They may understand that their teenage son comes home at all hours because he's trying to assert his independence from Mom and Dad. But what they can do about his lateness is an entirely different matter. Should they let him continue to do it? And what should they do when he simply ignores their rule that he be home by 11 o'clock?

That's where *The Family Contract* comes in. If you're the kind of parent who believes a 15-year-old kid shouldn't come wandering home at the crack of dawn on a school night, this book is for you. If you believe it's ultimately your responsibility to recognize the early warning signs of problems in your teen, this book will help. And, if you're the kind of parent who wants to do something about these problems starting right now, read on. (Then again, if you're that kind of parent, you might not need this book.)

HOME WORK

In their book *In Search of Excellence*, Tom Peters and Bob Waterman write that when you get on an airplane and notice coffee stains on the seat tray, it makes you worry about the engine maintenance. Forgive me for comparing your kids to Delta, but when you buy your preschooler seven packs of Rubba-Dubba Dental Destruction Fun Gum just because he throws a 120-decibel temper tantrum in the express checkout line, you have taken that first step toward "slipshod maintenance." In that one simple transaction, you have begun shaping a kid who, after proper training from another kid with hair spiked to resemble the Eiffel Tower, will soon be stealing your VCR to buy his weekly supply of "Ecstasy."

The scenario continues. Instead of Destruction Gum, it's destruction by drugs. Focused on finding reasonable, "civilized" solutions, you continue to look the other way, ignoring the "coffee stains" and replacing your VCRs on a monthly basis—creating a separate column on your computer spreadsheet expense report for "Unsolved Crime." Meanwhile, your kid inexplicably becomes so Ecstatic one night that he is discovered attempting to swim laps in the breakdown lane of Interstate 45.

Tough, but true—and more common than you might think. In both psychiatric hospital and outpatient settings, parents often ask me for help with a kid who is similarly "out of control." Therapy with kids is particularly difficult when they either don't show up for sessions or, cheerfully arriving for their first office visit, they pour hot coffee on your lap just for a laugh—their way of saying hello. For many of these families, help starts with denying their kids access to coffee, and continues with an application of the techniques described in this book. Parents who simply drop their kids off at the hospital or at my office with the idea that they'll pick them up after they are "fixed" or "straightened out" have a very long wait. The others—those who are willing to join the "treatment team" and participate actively in therapy—see the fastest and most stable results.

Listen to this story:

I recently met a man at a party who told me about his daughter. He said he was very proud of her. He and his wife had divorced when his daughter was about 10 and he had won custody of her. Despite the divorce, his daughter had gone on to make A's and B's throughout high school; she was presently working her way through college. He said that when she was a teenager she always came home at a reasonable hour and he never had to worry about her using drugs or alcohol.

I asked him what his secret was. He said he really didn't have any special parenting techniques and he guessed he was just lucky to have such a daughter. We changed the subject, and somehow we got to talking about cigarettes. He said that he didn't allow smoking in his house, and that he had made that very clear to his daughter years ago. To my surprise, he then rather casually added that if she had insisted on smoking, he would have told her to find someplace else to live.

He had not thought about any particular philosophy of

raising kids, but apparently he was fully prepared to throw his daughter out of the house for smoking a cigarette. This kind of parental attitude, though extreme, stands in stark contrast to parents who cower in fear and say nothing when their teenage darling "borrows" the family car, returns home drunk in the middle of the night, and punches a hole in the wall. Instead of firm, consistent action, they decide to have a "rap" with the boy when he awakens the next afternoon, hinting that he might have exercised better judgment. But before Dad can complete the first sentence, "Sleeping Beauty" regains semiconsciousness and is walking about the room looking for the car keys....

Does a seemingly harsh no-smoking policy have anything to do with why the man's daughter in the above example grew up to be a healthy, mature adult? Could be. Many of the parents I've seen over the years, like this particular father, have developed on their own ways of dealing with their kids, individualizing the general rules to fit the needs of their own particular family. In all fairness, I should point out that I learned quite a few good parenting techniques from them, too. This book is an effort to describe what we learned from each other over the years.

I must also point out one important "rider" to *The Family Contract*, namely that parenting—no matter how good—cannot prevent biologically based disorders such as schizophrenia or clinical depression from occurring. These conditions must be treated like any other medical condition. Nor can "bad parenting" be blamed completely for a teenager's problems; after all some pretty normal and successful teens and adults have grown up under the most difficult of circumstances. As a friend of mine once said, "Parents can't take too much credit—or too much blame—for their kid's success."

Nevertheless, "good parenting" beats "bad parenting" anytime. And this book (I hope) can help you become one of those good parents.

A BLUEPRINT FOR PARENTING

Think of this book as a set of instructions. (It might be a bit lengthy, but unlike 98 percent of all instruction booklets at least it's not in Japanese.)

The Family Contract's purpose is to help kids grow—emotionally, physically, and academically. We'll start with the "whys": why your teen might need help, why problems arise, and why family contracts work. We'll then move into the "nuts and bolts" of family contracts—writing one, fitting it into a daily routine, and keeping it happily enforced.

A healthy family environment doesn't just happen. It needs help from you. But together—you, me, *and* your teen—we can get through the "insane" teenage years intact, in control and in total confidence that a successful future is within your teen's reach.

Oh, yes. I almost forgot. Before you begin Part I (in English as promised), I have a favor to ask. As father to two teenagers, I've learned a few valuable parenting lessons, not the least of which is the educational value of mistakes. I wouldn't say they've been particularly difficult kids to raise (although at times Alyson and I have theorized that they might be reincarnations of Hittite chariot warriors.) Anyway, any mom or dad knows that portraying yourself as an "expert" on parenting to your kids carries a risk factor roughly equivalent to that of Sumo wrestling one day after a hernia repair. So, in a direct appeal to you, the reader, I'm asking that you help me keep this book from my kids. It includes all my best parenting tips but, until they both turn 18, it must remain classified.

Thanks for understanding.

CHAPTER ONE

A Family What?

It was a sunny, brisk October day, the kind of day when kids have other things on their minds than math and English grammar. Take 15-year-old Suzie. During fifth-period history, she passed her best friend, Lois, a note: "This is a drag. Let's cut the rest of the afternoon." Fifteen minutes later, they were headed for Suzie's house in a half-run, half-prance, impaired only by a crisp autumn wind that prevented them from lighting their Newport 100s.

Their illicit cigarettes at long last lit, they burst through the back door into the kitchen. Suzie grabbed a one-pound bag of potato chips from the cupboard, Lois picked up a paper plate to use as an ashtray, and, together, their arms full, they headed for the den to check out MTV.

As soon as they had flopped down on the sofa, Suzie jumped up again. "Forgot the Cokes. I'll be right back." Stuffing a handful of potato chips into her mouth, Suzie made her way back to the kitchen. But just as she yanked open the refrigerator door, she realized that something was different: her mom had cleared off all the stuff that usually decorated the door. Instead of coupons, tickets, and scribbled notes, the plastic fruit magnets held up some typed 8½" x 11" plain bond. It looked serious, like some kind of official document. Suzie merely shrugged; she was eager to get back to MTV. She grabbed two Cokes, slammed the refrigerator door with her foot, and had been about to turn away when something caught her eye. Slowly, she moved in for a closer look.

The document on the refrigerator door had her name on it.

Suzie yanked it off the door, the fruit magnets clattering to the floor. She glanced over its three pages, all neatly typed and stapled together. She uttered a loud profanity.

"What?" Lois shouted from the other room.

"Nothing," Suzie mumbled. She put the now forgotten Cokes on the kitchen counter and carefully read the entire first page of the document, from top to bottom.

THE THING POSTED ON
THE REFRIGERATOR DOOR

Here's what the first page said:

Family Contract for Suzie
The Most Important Rules

Breaking any of the following rules means going to Level One for at least a week:

- No cutting classes at school.
- No sneaking out of the house.
- No physical violence (hitting, kicking, throwing things, damaging property).
- No using drugs or alcohol—or seeing kids who use them.
- No cigarettes
- No lying to parents.
- No sexual acting out.
- Always must do what Mom and Dad say.

This had to be another one of her mother's corny ideas. Who could possibly enforce ridiculous rules like this? Besides, she only did some of this stuff occasionally; what's once in a while have to do with the bigger picture. Once in a while doesn't need to be punished. After all, Suzie only cut classes a couple of times this month—and she only sneaked out last week because Lois had broken up with her boyfriend and needed to see her. Sneaking out Saturday night couldn't possibly count; it was too important. It had been the night of Jaynie's party and Sam was going to be there. When her parents told her she couldn't go, Suzie had no other choice....

And what's this violence thing? Just because she threw some pillows around when she got mad doesn't mean there has to be a "rule" about it. Are her parents going to handcuff her from now on? And no beer or cigarettes? She might as well curl up into a ball and die.

Honestly. Suzie banged a Coke can on the countertop for emphasis. This thing had loopholes a mile wide. How would her mother and father even know when she was lying? At least all she told were "little white lies." Why upset them about detention or the time Miss Riley made her stay after school for disrupting the class?

But the last one really got to her. "Always must do what Mom and Dad say" was the corniest of them all. It sounded like a rule for a kindergarten kid—not a full-fledged teenager.

And what was this "Level One" nonsense, anyway? The entire thing was completely stupid—and best forgotten.

Suzie savagely crumpled the papers; she stuffed them into the garbage bag between a banana peel and some coffee grounds. She picked up the Cokes and went back to Lois and MTV, shaking her head all the while. "Family contract. I don't believe this. She's gotta be kidding."

But Suzie's mother wasn't kidding—and neither was her father. When the family all sat down to dinner later that same evening, her father gave her another shock. He produced, seemingly from thin air, a clean copy of the very same official document Suzie had rammed into the garbage a few hours earlier. A short, to-the-point discussion followed and, despite her misgivings, Suzie actually found herself signing her name to the bottom of the last page under her parent's watchful eyes:

> I, Suzie, have read the Family Contract, understand it, and am willing to try to follow it. I understand that in signing this contract, I might disagree with part of it or all of it, but I will follow the rules in it just the same.

| —————— | ———————— | —————— |
| Suzie | Dad | Mom |

This is outrageous, Suzie said to herself, crossing the fingers of her left hand as she signed with her right. If they seriously think I'm going to go along with this, they're even dumber than I thought. They must have just finished some book about how to raise the perfect child. She'd sign just to get them off her back; it would all blow over in a couple of days.

But it didn't "blow over." And her "dumb" parents proved they were very smart indeed....

CHORES? RULES? CURFEWS?

The family contract Suzie signed was three pages long, and if she thought the first page with its important rules was a joke, she only had to go on. The second page contained all the details about things Suzie *should* do. Her parents had written it together after much thought because they wanted certain aspects of her behavior to change. Here's what the second page of Suzie's family contract looked like:

Reading down the list, Suzie could see exactly where her parents were headed with this "point sheet." What they were willing to assign "points" for were all the things *they* cared about and she didn't care about at all—or at least not much, anyway. She could see they had put a lot of work into spelling out everything they normally either nagged or pleaded or yelled about.

As Suzie glanced over the page, she kept shaking her head in disbelief. She went over each category, one by one:

1. **Routine chores.** Suzie already fed Cookie her dinner every night—when she wasn't too busy watching TV or talking on the phone. She never made her bed; she never saw much point in it. After all, she'd only crumple up the sheets again the next night anyway. Besides, cleaning up was Mom's job.

Family Contract for Suzie
Week of _____

RULE	POINTS	S	M	T	W	Th	F	S
Routine chores (feed dog, clean room, dry dishes, etc.)	0–3							
Special chores (laundry, ironing, vacuuming, bathe dog, etc.)	0–3							
Curfew	0–2							
School								
On time	0–1							
Behavior	0–2							
Homework	0–5							
Practice piano	0–3							
Physical exercise, (aerobics, jogging, gymnastics)	0–3							
Read (book or newspaper—not school-related)	0–3							
Participate in school activities (soccer, yearbook, football games)	0–2							
Personal hygiene (dental floss, daily shower)	0–2							
General attitude and behavior	0–3							

DAILY TOTAL   — — — — — — —

WEEKLY TOTAL _____

2. **Special chores.** This was starting to look like a slave labor camp. Laundry and ironing were adult jobs. Suzie was confident her parents intended to pay her for vacuuming the house and giving Cookie a bath. Nobody would do those jobs for free.

3. **Curfew.** Since when did Suzie need a curfew. Didn't her parents trust her?

4. **School.** Let's get real. It was her father's job to wake her up in the morning and drive her to the bus stop. If Suzie was late getting to school, it was his fault—not hers. . . . Mmhmm. Behavior. That had to involve those things she kept under "little white lies." How could her parents actually ly check up on her? Surely they weren't in cahoots with her teachers or, heaven forbid, the principal. Homework, however, was a different story. Yes, they could check up on that. But they'd have to be fair. Six hours a day in school was enough. How could they expect her to go home and do even more work. Suzie had her own "important rule": Do as little homework as possible—and only when Mom and Dad are sitting right there and doing it with you.

5. **Practice piano** was another bone of contention. Suzie kind of liked to play, but practicing was too much trouble. Her mother's broken-record speech was that it was too expensive for her to keep having private lessons if she wasn't going to practice. As far as Suzie was concerned, the whole thing was one big guilt trip.

6. **Physical exercise** had to be her dad's idea. He was really into jogging and all that stuff. Sure, Suzie loved to dance, but she *hated* those stupid gym uniforms and tried to get out of exercise as much as possible.

7. **Read** came from her mom. It had to. She loved to read and was always nagging Suzie to go to the library, or look up this author, or listen to some passage or another. To tell you the truth, Suzie didn't really mind reading; it was just that she wasn't much in the habit. Watching TV was so much easier.

8. **Participating in extracurricular activities at school** was another subject for endless debate. Going to the yearbook meeting meant hanging around school the whole day. When the bell rang, all Suzie wanted to do was dash. If she went to this club and that event, she'd never have time to hang out with the guys at the coffee shop. She'd never see her boyfriend, Sam. And she'd have to spend all her time with "nerds." After all, weren't they the only "geeks" who did these things?

9. **Personal hygiene** made Suzie giggle. She took showers when she needed to and she used deodorant every day. But now that she had braces, her parents were trying to turn her into a fanatic about keeping her teeth clean. Flossing was totally unrealistic.

10. **General attitude and behavior** looked to her like some "catch-all" category. To Suzie, it smelled like a trap. She bet that every time she yelled at her mother or used a swear word at the dinner table they'd dock her a point—or however demerits in this system was supposed to work.

The whole thing stunk. But chances were there was no need to get worked up about it. They'd give up when they found out she just wouldn't go along with it. They'd forget the whole idea.

But despite her very best efforts to sabotage the deal, Suzie, like many other teens before her, did indeed "go along with it." Quite simply, she had to. She had already signed the family contract, and her parents were standing by her word—and theirs. . . .

Level Privileges

PRIVILEGE	LEVEL (by weekly point totals)			
	One (0–30)	Two (31–60)	Three (61–90)	Four (over 90)
Allowance (per week)	0	$1	$2	$5
Phone (minutes per day)	0	10	30	60
Special privileges (such as overnight guests, movies, gifts)	none	none	1/week	2/week
Television, video games	none	1 hr/day	1 hr/day on school days, 2 hrs/day on weekends	1 hr/day on school days, unlimited on weekends
Outside play	none	1 hr/day on school days, 3 hrs/day on weekends	2hrs/day on school days, 6 hrs/day on weekends	4 hrs/day on school days, unlimited on weekends
Bedtime	8:00 PM	8:30 PM	9:00 PM on school nights, 11:00 PM on weekends	10:00 PM on school nights, 1:00 AM on weekends
Unsupervised time	none	none	none on school days, 2 hrs/day on weekends	1 hr/day on school days, 5 hrs/day on weekends
Curfew	no outside time at all	6:00 PM	8:00 PM on school nights, 10:00 PM on weekends	9:00 PM on school nights, midnight on weekends

MAKING LIFE SIMPLER

As parents, you're probably wondering how to make these rules and regulations stick. Believe me, it has nothing to do with whips, chains, or abuse. But it has everything to do with the preceding page, entitled "Level Privileges":

Poor Suzie. She'd been so overcome from pages one and two that she'd barely looked at this page.

She should have, though, because that's where the big surprise came from at the end of the first week. Even though her parents had explained that she had to earn more than 30 points just to hoist herself out of the Level One category (and get some of her teenage privileges back), Suzie had carried on as usual. She never dreamed that her parents would actually follow through on this ridiculous family contract. She never believed for a minute that they would actually do the bookkeeping on this new system of theirs. So Suzie didn't change. She cut school on Monday, refused to walk the dog on Friday, and threw her clothes on her bedroom floor all week.

When the first Friday rolled around, Suzie's parents told her regretfully that she had earned a total of only nine points for the week.

"So what?" Suzie asked.

"So you're still on Level One," her dad answered. "Look at page three of the family contract. That means this coming week you get no allowance, you can't use the phone at all, you have to come directly home from school each day, you can't watch TV or even go outside. And, oh yes, it's lights out by eight P.M. every night."

"Right, Dad," Suzie said, trying not to panic. "No problem. But, ah, don't forget that Lois and I are going to the movies tonight. I'm supposed to sleep over at her house afterward."

"Sorry, Suzie," her mother explained. "You're on Level One."

"Mom...Dad? Hey, you can't do this to me." Suzie's face got red, then white. "Hey, wait a minute. This isn't fair. You can't just cancel my plans like that. You can't tell me what to do. You have no right to...Who do you think...What makes you think I'm going to..."

Suzie's stuttering fell on deaf ears. But it didn't stop her. At first she chafed at every single little task or chore she had to do to get "points" and earn privileges. She grumbled to herself—and to anyone unlucky enough to be near her—that this was a lousy system, that she felt like a prisoner, that a happy family life wasn't supposed to imitate life in the armed forces, that coercion was the tool of tyrants and she absolutely wasn't going to put up with this kind of indignity.

But it only took a couple of weeks for Suzie to get the idea. No completed tasks or good behavior, no points— and no points meant no privileges. This family contract was for real. So Suzie began to study the document in earnest. She began to figure out what she had to do to get enough weekly points for a $5.00 allowance, for telephone privileges, for TV time, for free time outside the house, for a respectable bedtime. Before long, she had the "Level Privileges" memorized.

Little by little, Suzie got used to this new way of life. So did her parents. By the end of the year they were accustomed to an orderly family life with a teenager who took care of her schoolwork and pulled her weight around the house. The obnoxious, spoiled, and undisciplined Suzie of the previous October had undergone a transformation right before their eyes. She had actually become a fairly reasonable human being, a teenager who acted in acceptable (if not always predictable) ways.

Of course, Suzie's parents were delighted with her improvement. But the surprising outcome of all this was the fact that Suzie, despite her outward show of resistance, was secretly pleased with the way life was going, too.

It was no miracle. Nor did it take heroic effort on anyone's part. All it took was the family contract.

Setting up a contract takes about three hours. Enforcing it required about 15 minutes a day. That's it.

THE PRINTED PAGE

The family contract is meant to be flexible. It's not etched in stone and it must be adapted to your lifestyle, your teen, and your family life. You have to use your imagination. If Suzie had been only 7 years old, her maximum allowance would have been one dollar a week. Had she been 17, one of the privileges would have been use of the family car. Had she been a boy, she would have worked toward more outside play—and less telephone time. Whatever. The privileges and chores, though they make life nicer in the present, don't really matter in the long run. What does matter are the family contract's intangibles, the benefits that will ultimately render it obsolete and superfluous. These benefits include:

- Trust
- Self-reliance
- Creative thought
- Good physical health
- Impulse control
- Frustration tolerance
- Responsibility
- Mature judgment

Over the years, many of the parents I've counseled have found the family contract a lot more appealing than pleading, nagging, and threatening. More effective, too. It simply and consistently sets up rules for behavior, lists certain privileges, and shows how a child can work toward these privileges in plain black and white—with a wiped-clean slate every week.

Now maybe you don't feel you need a family contract and that's fine. But if you think your child's behavior and attitude could stand improvement and if you're open to a new approach, the family contract could be the answer to your prayers. I've seen it work for children of all ages, but like all learned behavior, it is most effective if utilized early.

So, without further delay, let's go on to the facts you'll need to understand to make up your own family contract—why it works and how it works. Read on.

CLAUSE PAUSE
Do I Really Need a Family Contract in My House?

Look over the following statements. If you agree with more than two of them, a family contract can go far in making your "Home, Sweet Home":

1. My teenager refuses to clean her room—no matter what I say or do.
2. My son stays out half the night—and never gives me a good reason why.
3. My daughter talks on the phone day and night—and never gets her homework done.
4. My son is failing an important class.
5. My daughter's English teacher called me to complain about her absences in class—absences I know nothing about.
6. My son refuses to talk to me. He spends all his time in his room with the door closed—and the stereo blasting.
7. My daughter is always yelling at me. I always seem to provoke her without meaning to.
8. I found some marijuana in my son's desk drawer.
9. I don't like the crowd my teenager is hanging around with.
10. My daughter just announced that she's quitting school. She doesn't want to talk about college.
11. My son's stopped caring about the way he looks. He's sullen, sloppy, and dirty.
12. My teenager watches entirely too much TV—but I feel helpless to stop it.
13. My daughter just started smoking and refuses to listen to me when I tell her to stop.
14. My son hangs around the house when he's not at school. He doesn't go outside and he certainly doesn't get enough exercise.
15. Sometimes I feel like my teenager's maid. All I do is clean up, pick up, and every chore in between.

CHAPTER TWO

Why Make a Family Contract?

- According to the National Institute of Drug Abuse, approximately half our high school seniors are getting drunk on the average of every other week.
- One-sixth of recent high school graduates acknowledge having tried cocaine.
- There are around one million teenage pregnancies every year in America—and approximately one-third of these girls get no prenatal care.
- Teenage suicide rates have tripled since the 1950s to 5,400 per year.
- AIDS is the seventh leading cause of death in the 15-to-24-year-old age group.
- The National Commission Against Drunk Driving reports that a person under the legal drinking age is twice as likely to die in an alcohol-related crash as an adult over 21.
- High school teachers surveyed in the 1950s reported that the major problems they found among their students included tardiness, gum-chewing, and incomplete homework. By the 1980s, this list had changed considerably—to drug abuse, alcoholism, assault, and verbal threats of physical violence.
- Only 72 percent of kids in America graduate from high school.

As these statistics show, it's a dangerous world out there for our kids. Between MTV and the evening news, glitzy magazines and sobering headlines, a teen can get confusing messages—to say the least. In fact, teenagers today need their parents more than ever to offer firm guidance and draw specific boundaries between right and wrong.

Unfortunately, many parents leave this role to teachers— but schools can only do so much. It is virtually impossible for a teacher to get some kids to sit and listen in a regular classroom setting, much less actually learn anything—especially when there are about thirty other kids they must attempt to educate simultaneously. (Incidentally, the reward for the college-educated teacher who deals with mountains of paperwork and hordes of disrespectful and abusive students is the lucrative salary of $20,000 to $30,000 a year. In a country preparing to spend $518 million *per plane* for over 60 Stealth bombers and a *trillion*—you read it right, that's "t" as in "trillion"—dollars on Star Wars, it appears that our economic priorities have been set by Rambo.)

The pure and simple truth is that teachers are not parents—and they can't do the parents' job. A 1988 survey of 22,000 teachers by the Carnegie Foundation for the Advancement of Teaching found that 90 percent felt that a lack of parental involvement was a problem in their schools. They described their students as "emotionally needy" and "starved for attention and affection." Ernest Boyer, president of the Carnegie Foundation, said, "Teachers repeatedly made the point that in the push for better schools they cannot do the job alone, and yet there is a growing trend to expect schools to do what families, communities, and churches have been unable to accomplish."

THE NEW VERB

Parenting: it's become the buzzword of the 1980s and '90s—fraught with misleading information, inconsistency,

CLAUSE PAUSE

Does Mental Illness Run in Families?

Aristotle observed that "drunken women bring forth children like themselves." It has long been known that adults who abuse children are often victims of child abuse themselves. Many studies show the incidence of depression, manic-depressive illness, bulimia and anorexia nervosa to be higher in relatives of people with these conditions. But just because an illness appears more frequently in a family does not necessarily mean that it is inherited. Influenza, for example, is found to run in families because it is an infectious communicable disease. The only connection it has to "genes" are the soaking wet denim kind that kids put on in chilly weather and, hours later, come down with all-out colds.

and timidity on disciplinary issues. In all fairness, psychiatrists and psychologists might be partly to blame for this problem. Parents have been bombarded with warnings from mental health professionals that they must "understand" their child, that spanking is tantamount to child abuse, that they must "relate to the child" as a "buddy" or friend.

And there is some validity in this. Certainly a caring, understanding attitude in which a parent is able to place himself in his child's little shoes is crucial in raising a psychologically healthy child. Unfortunately, this message has become, for many parents, a distortion that says there is no place for rules or their enforcement in the home.

I recall a 7-year-old boy I was asked to evaluate for "school phobia" during my residency training. It seems the little boy wouldn't go to school. Grandma would drop him off at the schoolyard, but he would climb back in the car before she could pull away. She would then drive him home where he would spend the rest of the day eating ice cream and watching cartoons. Mom was exasperated. She complained—and I quote: "I wish they wouldn't show those darn cartoons on TV during school hours!"

While it is true that school refusal may represent serious emotional and/or learning disability problems in a child, this was not the case with this little boy. Nobody told him that just as there are rewards to be gained from attending school, there are punishments for skipping. He was not a sick child; he was, instead, essentially parentless. He had no firm hand guiding him. When I suggested to Mom that she might consider laying down the law to her son about school attendance, she protested. "But he'll get mad." It was as if his anger was to be avoided at all costs. After all, when he got mad he threw his toys around the room and slammed the doors, and Mom felt powerless to stop him....

Another mother I saw complained that she was exhausted from driving. It seems her 5-year-old son insisted that she drive by some oil refineries every morning on the way to school. We never did figure out why he wanted to see the refineries so much. True, they can be intriguing to look at, but there was one slight problem: the refineries were about 15 miles out of the way. Being a rather naive young doctor, I had to ask the obvious question. I was condescendingly told ("Don't you know anything, Mr. Expert?") that if she didn't comply with this demand, he would scream. Of course.

Yet another family told me they had actually chopped down a perfectly healthy tree in their front yard because they couldn't keep their son from climbing it. (This is a bit speculative, but when this kid begins robbing the local Stop and Go later in life, the parents might feel compelled to firebomb the entire convenience store.)

These real-life stories represent a sad state of affairs. Even sadder, I see similar situations in my practice all the time. Parents fear following their own good judgment about discipline. They fear being accused by therapists of being, at best, outdated and, at worst, child abusers if they enforce rules for their children at home. Yes, a 7-year-old child who knows no limits to his behavior is a big problem. But the reality is that this youngster will become a teen and, a few years down the road, a young adult—and a 20-year-old with this problem is truly frightening. A child's behavioral and emotional problems must be addressed early on. As Jesse Jackson so succinctly put it: "We must discipline the child while the child is a child."

But how? Sometimes parents genuinely just don't know what to do. It has always seemed ironic to me that we require licenses for everything from driving a car to fishing, but there is very little formal training available on parenting. We learn parenting from our parents. Parental skills and weaknesses tend to be passed on through the generations. For example, I learned the value of hard work and family loyalty from my parents. (However, I also grew up thinking that Lawrence Welk was the greatest musician in the history of civilization.)

Both 1988 presidential candidates (who presumably learned more skills than weaknesses from their parents) commented during their campaigns that the solution to problems with our kids lies beyond the scope of the government and our schools. The responsibility for kids lies with the parents, and while that may be a little scary for some, to most parents it will be a profound relief.

It is in this spirit that I offer the family contract. I won't say it's the perfect solution and that it works in every case. But I will say it goes a long way in helping communication between you and your teen, in guiding him or her in healthy, productive, and positive ways—and in preventing the all-pervasive peer culture that surrounds teenagers from becoming the *only* powerful influence in your child's life.

The pull of these negative peer cultures usually lead to self-destruction—either through drugs, promiscuity, suicide, or violence. Unfortunately, these dangers have a very real place in our children's world. Let's go over each of

CLAUSE PAUSE

AIDS Test

In an April 1988 study of 1,153 Southern California college students, Dr. Stuart Oskamp discovered that they gave the correct answers to questions about AIDS 88 percent of the time. But when these same students were asked about taking precautions for safe sex, *only 25 percent said they were.*

In another college survey undertaken by Susan Cochran, Ph.D., 47 percent of the men and 60 percent of the women reported that they had been told a lie in order to have sex. In turn, 20 percent of these same men and 4 percent of the women said they would falsely claim they had taken the AIDS test and gotten a negative result. (These same figures elicit chest pains in 98 percent of surveyed parents.)

these now—and see how a family contract can circumvent tragedy.

THE DEADLY MIX: KIDS, DRUGS, AND ALCOHOL

Although declining, the use of alcohol and drugs continues to be widespread among young people—despite our best intentions. Here's proof: The Parents' Resource Institute for Drug Education (PRIDE) conducted a survey of 203,000 students in grades 6–12 during the 1987–88 school year. Their results? 58 percent of the boys and girls drank beer, 56 percent drank wine coolers, 46 percent drank hard liquor, 35 percent smoked cigarettes, 20 percent used marijuana, and 4 percent had tried cocaine. And, of the high school students who drank, a full 30 percent reported that they usually got drunk when they did imbibe.

Drug and alcohol abuse are rather complicated issues, involving biological, hereditary, psychological, cultural, and stress-related components. But do notice that I said "complicated"—not impossible. There are fundamental rules governing substance abuse prevention that parents can include in the family contract and, better yet, enforce. Because of the dangerous, far-sweeping ramifications of drug and alcohol abuse for our future as a society, I'm devoting all of Chapter Nine to this subject.

SEX AND THE SINGLE TEEN IN AN AIDS-THREATENING WORLD

Listen to Dr. Antonia Novello in a December 1988 report to the Secretary of Health and Human Services: "The official figures* include only those children whose condition was reported to the Centers for Disease Control (CDC). Probably for every child who meets the CDC definition of AIDS, another two to ten are infected with HIV. It is estimated that by 1991 there will be at least 10,000 to 20,000 HIV-infected children in the United States."

The 1988 International Symposium on AIDS in Stockholm reported that virtually 100 percent of people infected with the virus go on to develop the disease. AIDS itself is, of course, universally fatal. For those who don't already know, AIDS is always fatal. I must also inform these people that the Beatles are no longer together.

Pardon the sarcasm, but it becomes an occupational hazard. I was talking with a 17-year-old kid the other day who was telling me about a fun night he had last week. He was riding around in his pickup truck when he heard a car horn. Unbelievably, he came eye to eye with

---

* At the time of this report there had been 1,291 reported cases of AIDS in children under 13 and an additional 325 cases in the 13-to-19-year-old age group.

a beautiful woman in the next lane honking at him. He had sex with her the next night. Saving the best news for last, he told me she was 21—which meant to him that she was extremely sexually experienced. I asked him if he knew about AIDS and he reassuringly told me that he knew it was fatal and that you could contract it sexually. However, he had not used a condom. Why not? "I asked her if she had it [AIDS] and she said she didn't. She told me some other real personal things about herself and I don't think she would lie to me about something like that." Of course not. He had known her for an entire two-day period by then so they had reached the depths of intimacy comparable only to, perhaps, Mickey and Minnie. I gently pointed out to him that she might be a carrier and not know it. People who pick their sexual partners on the freeway have been known to make subtle tactical errors from time to time. He didn't think so. (With all due respect, Bill Cosby refers to kids in this age bracket as "brain damaged.")

We used to warn teenagers about the risks of casual sex with the usual parental proclivity for conveying a double message: "Don't do it, but if you do at least be discreet and keep it to yourselves." Before AIDS, the risks included venereal disease, pregnancy, and premature teen marriages. Today, however, parents are compelled to break down whatever embarrassment or resistance they might have to discussing sexuality with their children because this now literally represents a life-and-death issue.

The fact is that kids and adolescents tend to see themselves as invulnerable. *They* won't get pregnant. *They* won't come down with AIDS. *They* won't die. To quote a song from the movie *Fame*, "I'm gonna live forever!" Death is too abstract, illness too remote to conceptualize, and teenage pregnancy or infectious disease drops in on other kids—not them. Teens tend not to read the Center for Disease Control statistics on AIDS and, even if they did, it would be "boring" to look at numbers in a scientific paper. Only when their friends tragically die before their mid-twenties from AIDS will

CLAUSE PAUSE

Burnin' Down the School

Businessman H. Ross Perot recently said that "We're paying more than any other nation on earth [$328 billion] for educating our young people—and we have the least to show for it." He added that only about 20 percent of mothers were available to tutor their children at home. What Mr. Perot touched upon is more than an "education crisis." It is, at a more fundamental level, a "parenting crisis." Here's some mind-boggling news with vast implications for the "3 R's"—and all our futures:

- A 1988 Gallup Poll reported one in every seven adults cannot find America on a map. Seventy-five percent of American adults cannot find the Persian Gulf on a map. And another 61 percent cannot locate Massachusetts.
- The National Assessment of Educational Progress reported that only about 7 percent of 17-year-olds are adequately prepared for college-level science courses. They also found that American ninth-graders rank 14th out of 15 countries in science. In fact, American high school students in advanced science classes ranked dead last in biology.
- When asked whether the earth goes around the sun or the sun around the earth, 21 percent of 2,041 surveyed adults replied incorrectly. Another 7 percent simply didn't know.

they begin to understand the horror of what we are about to encounter in coming years.

Trusting the judgment of a child on issues of sexual behavior (or substance abuse or depression for that matter) is tantamount to neglect. Parents must trust their own judgment and the judgment of consulting professionals when necessary. They must have the conviction to enforce their intuition on how to be a mom or dad, even over the most vociferous objections of their kids. That's where the Family Contract comes in. As you will see in Chapter Three, it's a valuable tool in teaching your children specific behaviors, including responsibility for themselves and for those whom they come in contact with—intimately or not.

VIOLENT BEHAVIOR

The "What came first? The chicken or the egg?" school of thought loses steam when it comes to violence. It just doesn't matter. The bottom line, pure and simple, is this: If we don't enforce rules with our kids, the police eventually will. According to the Federal Bureau of Justice, the federal and state prison inmate population grew by 4 percent in the first six months of 1988 to a record 604,824. From 1980 to 1988, the number of female prisoners increased by a whopping 130 percent—to 30,834. The number of male prisoners increased by "only" 81 percent—to 573,990. (In the ·1950s, the *entire* prisoner population stood at around 50,000.) And, incidentally, 85 percent of these prisoners are in jail for drug- and alcohol-related crimes.

Another sobering statistic from the Federal Bureau of Justice: There are currently 237 prisoners serving time in our jails for every 100,000 U.S. residents—with many of the violent crimes coming from the teenage group.

One possible reason for this disturbing fact comes from our television tubes. Surveys show that three-quarters of our high school senior population watch television every day—but only half of them read books, magazines, and newspapers on a daily basis. In fact, the average American kid has spent 15,000 hours in school by the time high school graduation rolls around—but has watched approximately 18,000 hours of television during that same period. (It should be noted that this figure, roughly translated, means viewing approximately 10,000 television murders and other assorted acts of violence. Those who think that these statistics are unrelated to skyrocketing rates of violent crime and illiteracy among our youth also probably videotape episodes of *Wheel of Fortune* so they can be enjoyed again and again.)

More proof? A woman I know has two daughters who were *both* valedictorians in their respective classes. Her secret was that she had no TV set in her home.

Dangerous or not, TV is here to stay—but it can be turned to your advantage. A potent privilege, TV watching can be used as a reward for reaching a certain level as outlined in the family contract. And, by specifying how many hours your teen can watch the tube, you're helping to cut down on all that violence and mind-numbing MTV.

TEENAGE ANGST

It stands to reason that if we lived in a perfect world, our teenagers would grow up perfectly strong and healthy. But we don't—and we must look beyond black-and-white logic for answers. A recent study found that a fairly accurate knowledge of AIDS did not reduce high-risk sexual behavior among college students. Similarly, it's been found that a school's drug education programs alone won't stop drug abuse. Yet other research has found that certain types of suicide prevention education efforts may actually increase the risk of teenage suicide.

Clearly, the problems of self-destructive kids, as with adults, transcend purely intellectualized and "logical" reason, and enter the realm of the psychological. More specifically, teenagers, like adults, can be depressed.

It's very possible that acting in self-destructive ways is an indicator that your teenager is suffering from depression. The adolescent who drinks a six-pack of beer, who smokes a couple of joints, who goes tearing down the freeway at 90 miles an hour in the name of "fun," or who

CLAUSE PAUSE

No More Gum-Chewing in the Halls

So you used to think that chewing gum and talking out of turn were the worst things you could do in school. Well, times have definitely changed. Listen to this quote from the December 3, 1988 *Houston Chronicle*:

> The Houston school district will spend $483,600 in the next six months to employ police officers and boost security to lessen school violence, which Superintendent Joan Raymond said is at an all-time high.
>
> At a board meeting Friday, trustees approved Raymond's recommendation, which calls for placing off-duty police part-time on 20 secondary campuses, including some middle schools, and creating two special security teams.
>
> Raymond said that she has received more reports of violence on campus in the past two months than at any time in her two-year tenure.
>
> "I think [the incidents] are mostly fights and assaults," Raymond said. "We have been getting more teacher assaults, I must tell you. We are getting more knifings, stabbings, and assaults."
>
> Raymond's plan calls for creation of a "disruption response team" consisting of eight uniformed Houston Independent School District guards who will be trained in bomb search techniques, riot control, drug investigation, and weapons control.

has behavioral or academic problems in school could very well be in the throes of childhood depression and, on careful questioning, have several other of its symptoms.

The *DSM-III-R*, the diagnostic manual used by most psychiatrists and psychologists in the United States, lists several symptoms for "Major Depressive Disorder," including:

- Sleep disturbance—usually difficulty staying asleep during the night and early morning
- Decrease in appetite—usually accompanied by weight loss
- Lowered energy
- Impaired ability to concentrate
- Suicidal thoughts

As with adults, it is now understood that depression in children and adolescents can be caused by a combination of physical and psychological factors. Impaired thyroid gland function, for example, can lead to all the symptoms of depression described above. Why? It all has to do with the brain's biochemistry. A deficiency in thyroid hormone can affect the way other chemicals in the brain function.

In fact, there are two brain chemicals that have been proven to be closely linked with depression: norepinephrine and serotonin. Studies have found that a low level of serotonin accompanied by a low level of norepinephrine can cause depression. But because norepinephrine's chemical structure is similar to that of adrenaline, low serotonin levels combined with high norepinephrine levels can result in manic-depressive illnesses.

But the combination of biological and psychological factors are only two-thirds of the story. Environment—or stress—is yet another. In the strict medical definition, stress simply describes change. In their famous 1950s study of stress, Holmes and Roche were able to find a relationship between stress and illness. Not surprisingly, death of a spouse was ranked as the most severe life stress. But there were some unexpected findings. Changes that were perceived as good and positive (such as a job promotion) were also considered stressful—and predisposed people to medical problems.

The fact is that stress, like DNA, seems to affect our body and our brain chemistry. If we measured norepinephrine levels in the spinal fluid of someone in a life-threatening situation, the results would be vastly different from those levels found in a relaxed person. The same holds true for depressed people. Dr. Steve Targum, a psychiatric researcher at a Sarasota, Florida hospital, found changes in the white blood cells (the cells responsible for fighting off viruses and bacteria) of depressed patients—which could have important implications in studying the relationship between psychological state and resistance to infection. In effect, we could say that our body chemistry affects our ability to cope with stress—and stress affects our body chemistry.

This body chemistry is programmed by our genes, which are actually strands of DNA. Simply put, DNA is nature's "software"; its coding regulates not only our bodies, but our minds. More specifically, DNA regulates the chemicals in the brain, such as those before-mentioned "buddies," norepinephrine and serotonin—both of which are directly related to depressive disorders.

Because we inherit our DNA coding, mental disorders can run in families. Studies of identical twins have found that when one twin suffers from a major depression, so will the second twin—76 percent of the time. And, when twins are not raised in the same household, the figure only drops to 67 percent, proving that genes can be more powerful than a stressful environment.

On the other hand, you can also understand how a child raised by a chronically depressed parent might also become depressed without any hereditary push. A depressed parent might be less emotionally available to nurture the child. He might be more prone to temper outbursts, even violence. She might ignore the child's tears.

Mental health professionals have been debating this "nature versus nurture" controversy for years, with no definitive answers yet in sight. Instead, modern psychiatry subscribed to a more "holistic" view, using a "biopsychosocial" model of mental disorders—the biological, psychological, and social (or stress and environmental) factors that, taken together, can create mental illness. Here's an example:

If a child is born into a family with a strong history of diabetes, that child will be at increased risk for developing diabetes. But diabetes is not necessarily in the cards. As opposed to eye color, for instance, diabetes is not preordained. And should the illness develop, the severity depends not only on family genes, but on diet and exercise as well. In fact, intense power struggles often develop between parents and diabetic children about sticking to a diet and taking insulin. Here, a "purely medical" condition takes on clear psychiatric overtones, and in some cases, family therapy becomes as important as insulin in ensuring a child's health.

Depression is another example. A child born to a mother who is chronically depressed might be predisposed to depression. But it is the accompanying stress of having an emotionally unavailable and unnurturing parent that triggers the child's depression—not the gene pool. A bad test score, a rejection from the cheerleading squad, a marital breakup—all can play a part in bringing depression in a vulnerable, high-risk teen to the surface.

We can't reprogram our genetic structure (at least, not yet.) But, as a product of psychological and stress-related problems, depression can be stopped from overtaking your child—thanks to a family contract. A teen who reaches a weekly goal will undoubtedly get a confidence boost. Routines that become a part of daily life breed needed family security. Performance that only gets better thanks to the elimination of bad habits will make everyone happy.

Think of the family contract as a preventive measure— stopping depression from getting out-of-hand and resulting in...

THE SPECTER OF SUICIDE

We've all heard that teenagers seek guidelines even though they make a show of rebelling. Too much laissez-

---

CLAUSE PAUSE

Something You Need to Know About Sex

A surprising number of parents have no idea if their children are sexually active. Here's another surprising fact:

According to a 1988 Mark Clements Research, Inc. survey of 303 teenagers, two-thirds of America's 11 million teenage boys have had sex with a girl. On the average, their first sexual experience was at 15 and, by 18, they had had sex with an average of five girls.

---

faire parenting without the benefit of a family contract's discipline just might have created a whole generation of insecure, depression-prone teens. Not only has teenage suicide become a frightening new trend in today's confusing world, but it has become less an isolated incident and more a part of what is called the "cluster suicide" phenomenon.

A stark example comes from Westchester County, New York, where 10 adolescents committed suicide in 1984. Direct social contacts among the victims could not be proved, but there was evidence that those who died later had all read or heard about the earlier suicides.

Another example: In Plano, Texas, a prosperous, rapidly growing suburb of Dallas, eight teenager suicides were reported between February 1983 and February 1984. In Clear Lake, Texas—a Houston suburb—yet another teen cluster suicide recently occurred.

These suicide "clusters" bring up a major concern: Did the publicity around the events contribute to the problem? Some people accused the press of romanticizing the victims by publishing detailed biographical sketches and providing dramatic coverage of the mourning families and friends. They feared that this kind of coverage reinforced other kids' subliminal wish that suicide would provide the attention they so desperately desired. Indeed, a study by Dr. David P. Phillips reported a 12 percent increase in the national suicide rate in the month after Marilyn Monroe killed herself. He also found that there was a significant increase in single-car crashes following front-page suicide reports. Even more telling is the fact that the average age of the car-crash fatalities and the publicized suicide victims matched.

Although the irreversibility of death is obvious to any healthy adult, it isn't always understood by troubled teens. Publicity over suicides can, unfortunately, encourage adolescents' "magical thinking" that suicide can be a route to immortality and fame.

But publicity is one thing and talk is another. When discussed by parents, teachers, and qualified mental health professionals in a serious, nonjudgmental and nonsensationalized way, the sad statistics of teenage suicide tell us that we should worry only about not discussing it enough.

Here's proof: A study by a suicide prevention center in San Mateo County, California found that out of several hundred high school seniors, 12 percent had attempted suicide at least once—and *52 percent* had considered it seriously enough to actually plan the suicide. In another survey, the majority of college freshmen reported that they had a friend talk to them about committing suicide.

Indeed, many suicidal teens will confide in a friend— but they also make the friends promise to keep the news confidential. A good friend will, of course, try to talk the suicidal teen out of it—but this is usually ineffective. Worse, a good friend might keep quiet about the teen's problem out of misguided loyalty. Suicide prevention programs can successfully break this powerful and ultimately destructive bond. With suicidal thoughts so prevalent in today's teenage society, these preventive programs can make all the difference between life and death, resulting in lower suicide rates.

OTHER CROSSES A PARENT
OF A TEENAGER MUST BEAR

Woody Allen once said that life is divided into the horrible and the miserable. The "horrible" includes people with leprosy, terminal cancer, and quadriplegia. The "miserable" are everyone else. If we have somehow escaped the above-mentioned "horribles" of parenting (including AIDS, teenage suicide, and drug or alcohol addiction), there are enough "miserables" around to keep us company:

An item on every parent's "miserable" list includes those agonizing nights of wondering where our kids are when they're four hours late coming home. Then there's the experience of bailing our kids out of jail for DWIs so many times we're offered a frequent felony plan by the friendly folks at Jiffy Bail Bond Company. Another one? How about the misery of getting a mid-day call from the school counselor reporting that our son offered a bong-hit to the vice principal. The list goes on....

If the sobering issues mentioned in this chapter aren't quite enough to make every parent want to stand up and say, "Give me a family contract today!" here's one final note:

As I mentioned in the Introduction, my daughters really got into the family contract with a vengeance. Though their complaints were loud and verbally imaginative, they still washed the dog and cleaned the bathroom by the end of the first week. But there's even better news. After one month, they'd also improved their grades, their confidence at home and at school, and their disposition—even in the morning. They were acting responsible—and happy.

In today's complex world, I couldn't ask for more. Nor can I think of any better testament for the family contract. So, without any further ado, let's go on to the specific reasons *why* the contract works—and how it will work for you and your teen.

And I promise, no more statistics—at least for the next chapter or two.

CHAPTER THREE

Rules and Behavior

Billy had already had one run-in with the police. He drank on weekends and he hung around with a wild group of guys. Enough was enough and his parents instituted a family contract. Three months later, Billy is a different teen.

• Tracey had always been a bright child, bringing home A's and B's from school. But everything changed when she entered seventh grade. Suddenly, the sweet, polite girl her parents knew and loved turned into a screaming, wild-looking monster. Suddenly, they could do no right. If they told her to get off the phone and do her homework, they were cramping her style. If they told her to eat her dinner, they were invading her space. If they told her to open her bedroom door, they were told, in no uncertain terms, to leave her alone. If they asked her to walk the dog, they were met with chilling silence. At the end of their rope, Tracey's parents went to see a family therapist; they learned how a family contract could help get rid of their daughter's negative behavior, while it reinforced good manners, good grades, and good feelings. Today, everyone in the family (especially the now well-walked Fido) is happy.

• Jaime's mother believed in reason. When he took the family car and drove off, she tried to explain why he shouldn't do it. When he began to smoke cigarettes, she tried to tell him it was bad for his health. But when Jaime began to drink and get into trouble at school, she finally put her foot down. No more explanations. No more reasoning. From now on it would be a family contract, smoothly enforced and consistent.

Call it a fad. Call it a parent effectiveness training tool. Call it a lot of psychobabble. Whatever you call it, the family contract works. In fact, it's based on common sense—which has been around for a long, long time. I didn't invent the idea of a family contract. Good parents and good family therapists have been using it for years—without labels, without pigeonholes, and sometimes without even being aware of it.

But common sense alone is not enough to make a family contract work. The reason why it can be enforced so effectively has to do with the four basic principles of behavioral psychology called "operant conditioning"—four basic ways of changing behavior that have been around almost as long as that proverbial common sense.

How does "operant conditioning" work? Easy. Suppose we wanted to train a horse to turn to the left. (Before I hear any protests that we are smarter than horses, I would direct the reader to sit through three hours of prime-time network TV. Speaking from experience, sugar cubes begin to start sounding pretty good.) The four principles could be described as follows:

1. **Positive reinforcement.** Give the horse a sugar cube if he happens to turn to the left.
2. **Negative reinforcement.** Take away the horse's sugar cube if he happens to turn to the right.
3. **Aversive conditioning.** Whip the horse if he decides to turn to the right.
4. **Extinction.** Ignore the horse completely until he turns to the left.

Of these four principles, positive reinforcement has the best record of success. The lure of positive reinforcement, for example, has netted Las Vegas approximately $800 million in the time it's taken you to read this paragraph. (You don't hear about horses dropping that kind of money, now do you?)

That's it. These four principles of behavior lay the foundation for every family contract. But before we go on and actually construct a contract that you can start using right now, there's one more stop. It's one involving your teen's personality—and three character disorders that can unleash behavior sabotaging the best-laid contract.

WALK WITH PERSONALITY

If there is any common theme to link the rising rates of suicide, car accidents, violent crime, drug abuse, alcoholism, teen pregnancy, runaways, AIDS, and poor school performance among American youth, it probably isn't Red Dye #2. Assuming primary medical and psychiatric disorders have been ruled out, these problems might relate to one of three disorders of personality, defined in the *DSM III-R* as Borderline Personality Disorder, Narcissistic Character Disorder (NCD), and Sociopathic Personality Disorder. Let's go over each one now:

1. If I can't have you, no one can or, Borderline Personality Disorder

Thanks to Glenn Close's character in the recent movie *Fatal Attraction*, Borderline Personalities have achieved a certain amount of notoriety. But the disorder had been first diagnosed in the late 1940s, when pioneering physicians Otto Kernberg and Jules Masterson used the term for patients on the border between psychosis and neurosis.

(Sorry, but sometimes jargon is the only way to explain things. This won't take too long....)

People suffering from a *psychosis*, like schizophrenics, lose touch with reality. They will hallucinate, hearing voices or suffering from a delusion—such as staunchly believing the CIA is tapping their telephone. *Neurotics*, on the other hand, live in the real world—but not happily. They suffer from anxiety, depression, phobias, and obsessions. At first glance, Borderlines appear to be simply neurotic, but when they are subjected to stress, they become psychotic.

And speaking of stress, what is considered a traumatic situation for a healthy adult is different for Borderlines. They live from crisis to crisis. They get into fist fights at the bar. They break up with their lovers twice a week. They cut you off on the freeway while making obscene gestures.

To Borderlines, just the experience of solitude can produce anxiety—and even terror. They feel so panicky that they immediately seek out people—which is what the trendy new buzzword "codependency" is all about. While most people welcome private time, Borderlines avoid it with a vengeance.

Other symptoms include:

- Poor frustration tolerance.
- A chronic and persistent angry mood.
- Poor impulse control—often characterized by alcohol and drug abuse, suicidal gestures, "one-night stands," temper tantrums, and even physical violence.
- A tendency to see people in "black and white," in which others are either for them or against them. Period.
- Difficulty seeing both sides of an issue.

2. Me, Myself, and I or, Narcissistic Character Disorder (NCD)

Here's a typical NCD in action:

Joe is busy monopolizing the conversation to tell you how smart he was in purchasing his new BMW. But he explodes in anger when you interrupt him to tell him you have to go. You have to pick up your kid from school. Joe doesn't want to hear it. It won't hurt your kid to wait 10 more minutes. He just wants to finish this story—and if you were a "real friend," he wouldn't have to point that out....

Dr. Heinz Kohut is probably most widely credited for developing the concept of Narcissistic Character Disorder, which is characterized by:

- Grandiosity.
- Lack of empathy—an ability to imagine oneself in another's shoes and actually feel some of what he or she is feeling.

- A sense of entitlement.
- Intense anger when that sense of entitlement is supposedly infringed upon.

3. That's how I feel. Honest. Or, Sociopathic Personality

These people essentially have no conscience—which makes them sound so convincing. Stealing, lying, and cheating doesn't bother them in the least. Even more frightening, many Sociopaths have sadistic tendencies.

In a strictly technical sense, these three disorders pertain only to adults. It is not correct to apply them to adolescents and children. But I have a feeling that people's personalities don't suddenly change on their eighteenth birthday. In fact, I believe we are raising a generation of Borderlines, NCDs, and Sociopaths. Some studies estimate that as much as 15 percent of the general population carry at least one of these diagnoses—and I feel this figure is dramatically on the rise.

Interesting, you say. But what has this got to do with a family contract? Plenty. These disorders, unlike depression or other mental illnesses, have little to do with genes or body chemistry. They take root, at least in part, by impaired or negligent parenting. Further, unlike people with depression, the person with a personality disorder does not recognize that he has a problem within himself. He is unmotivated to change. The Borderline sees no problem in cursing out the kid working the counter at MacDonald's because he put too much ketchup on his burger. The NCD can't see why his girlfriend got so angry because he was forty minutes late and didn't call. ("Couldn't she understand that he had to see the end of the football game on TV? What's the big deal? Women!") The Sociopath feels that his criminal end justified his means because that's the "law of the jungle" and people who don't understand that are just plain stupid.

This tendency to "externalize" problems makes treatment nearly impossible. It's difficult *at best* to treat people for a problem when they don't feel they have a problem. Therapists must often wait until the behaviors

---

CLAUSE PAUSE

If There's a Problem, Change the Problem

Despite behavioral conditioning inroads, despite advances in medicine, psychotherapy, and science, many American corporations chose to fix a problem by attempting to work around it. This process is described by the elegant term "Dumbing Down." You may have noticed, for example, that at some of the fast food restaurants, the cash register has pictures of food on the buttons rather than words. (When computerization and robotics have totally taken over all intellectual functioning on earth, we're going to have to figure out what to do with a lot of spare time and no money. Personally, I'm planning on working on my behind-the-back frisbee catch.)

---

associated with these disorders cause secondary problems—such as trouble with the law, medical complications of substance abuse, and physical injury. Then, and sometimes only then, patients will be willing to admit they need therapy.

Obviously, if your teen refuses to believe he has a problem, he won't seek help—and he'll also be extremely resistant to any plans you have to initiate a family contract. ("What for? I don't need it! There's nothing wrong with me!") In fact, if your teen is suffering from any one of these three disorders, enforcing your family contract will be the equivalent of driving a Mack truck up a steep hill in an ice storm. It just won't work—despite your best intentions. These particular disorders require professional help.

But for now, it's time to move on and begin to put what you've learned into action. It's time to discover the nuts and bolts of a family contract.

CHAPTER FOUR

The Framework of the Family Contract

Constructing a family contract can seem overwhelming. "Where do I start? What are the most important things I want my teen to learn? When do I find the time to put pen to paper? How do I get him to do his share? What if I put too much emphasis on the wrong things? What if it doesn't work..." Before you've even begun, you're frazzled and unsure. As that little professor said in the movie *Yellow Submarine*, "So much to know, so little time."

That's where this chapter comes in. Think of it as a time-cutting, easy-to-follow recipe that's done much of the legwork for you. Here, you'll find all the nuts and bolts you need to write your own contract. All you have to do is fill in the blanks with your own individual and family needs.

To help you on your way, I've added some samples throughout this chapter, including different privilege/reward pages for ages 5 to 10, 10 to 15, and 16 to 18. But, as you browse through them, it's important to remember that when it comes to human personality, one size does not fit all. Simply photocopying the sample contracts will do you—and your child—no good. A sample doesn't take into account your child's age, size, talents, skills, limitations, and interests. It doesn't have room for your capability to enforce rules—or provide specific rewards and privileges. Use these samples—and this whole chapter—only as the guides they were meant to be.

It is far more effective to help people, as Jesse Jackson so eloquently stated, "on the front end of life instead of the back end of life." Therefore, the younger the child, the easier it is to make the family contract work. On this note, then, let's start without any further ado. There is no time like the present—and no better place to help than at home.

A CONTRACT THAT WORKS

A good family contract consists of four components: rules, points, levels, and privileges. Let's go over each one now:

The Golden Rules

These are the chores, the responsibilities, and the behavior that separates a good kid from a bad one. Each rule is worth a certain number of points. For every rule that is kept, your teen will receive points—which are translated into privileges.

●"The Most Important Rules"

These are the rules that must not be broken.

Think of the ten commandments imprinted in stone and you won't be far wrong about this list. Just as Moses handed them down from the mountain, so you, the parents, must hand them down to your teen as law. Without these rules, the rest of the contract simply won't work. In fact, they are so important and so integral to the dynamics of the family contract that they are the only rules that are not awarded points. Quite simply, they depict nonnegotiable fundamental behavior that sets kids, as a species, slightly apart from pit bulls.

To illustrate why compliance with these Important Rules is not rewarded, here's a story one of my professors told me many moons ago:

He had been treating a young girl with severe anorexia nervosa; she'd recently refused to eat altogether. After weeks of therapy, she came running down the hall to him one morning, proclaiming that she had eaten her entire breakfast. "Isn't that *wonderful*!?" she exclaimed. He responded with a nonchalant, "Oh, really?" and kept on walking. By not joining in the celebration and by responding in a matter-of-fact way, he intended to convey that eating a bowl of Cheerios needs to be distinguished from winning the Nobel Prize. The reward for complying with "The Most Important Rules" is the opportunity to be a member of the human race—nothing more and nothing less.

In addition to introducing your teen to civilization, The Most Important Rules also keep your contract running smoothly. In the same way a smoke alarm prevents fire, The Most Important Rules prevent such self-destructive actions as drug abuse or sexual promiscuity from running amuck, sabotaging the best-laid plans—and negatively affecting attitudes, behaviors, and emotions.

If and when your teen breaks any of these rules, you must begin emergency procedures. Privileges should be taken away immediately for a specific amount of time (for example, demotion to Level I for one week) and, if the behavior continues, it would be wise to seek professional help.

There are no exceptions to the Most Important Rules, but they can be bent, if necessary. "No physical violence," for example, might be difficult for a child who can't express anger any other way. But rather than abandoning the family contract, try giving the child permission to hit a mattress or a punching bag when angry.

The remaining rules below all receive points:

●Routine Chores

These are the elements that make the contract function on a daily basis. Cleaning his room, making her bed, mowing the lawn, washing the dishes or the car,

---

CLAUSE PAUSE

Level Four Doors

To help your kids see that Level Four privileges are not only desirable, but *accessible*, walk through a typical day, explaining what chores and rules would generate this level when points are tallied up at the end of the week. Voice confidence that your kids can achieve and maintain a Level Four consistently.

Establishing this expectation is a vote of confidence in them. In fact, during the crucial first contract week, give your children the benefit of the doubt and allow them Level Four privileges for seven days—until point-totaling day.

---

bathing the dog—whatever chores you feel are necessary to keep your household running smoothly should be put here. Remember, these chores are designed to teach your teen responsibility and self-confidence. The list should not be either too short (which won't teach your teen anything but a way to "pull the wool over your eyes") or too long (which will ultimately discourage her and make her dream of Cinderella).

●Special Chores

What separates these from the routine? They're not done as often—or they're projects that the entire family's been avoiding for several seasons in a row. In this category you might put doing the ironing, cooking dinner, cleaning the garage or attic, painting the house, landscaping, or polishing the furniture. What makes special chores nice are the fact that everyone can be involved. Family members can all participate and feel the satisfaction of a job well done.

●Curfew

Needless to say, this is one of the more unpopular items—but an absolutely necessary evil. Here, you not only detail the time you want your teen home on weekends and school nights, but the specific time when he or she must be in bed *with the lights out*. One important note: Don't paint yourself in a corner by requiring that your children be "asleep" by a certain time. They will soon insist (quite accurately) that they can't make themselves fall asleep by, say, ten o'clock.

Curfews can be modified from week to week—either later as a reward or earlier as a punishment.

●School Rules

When your kids are at school, it's the teachers' turn. You get to do all the things you hadn't had time to do before (such as creating a family contract). But there are certain school goals you can help your child attain— as you better prepare them to learn. These include punctuality, attendance, and behavior. Is he awake and ready for school? Has she completed all her morning preschool activities in time—including bathing and making lunch?

●Homework

This one's self-explanatory, but do make sure you've reviewed it before the next school day. (Note that I said "reviewed," not "done by." You've already done fifth grade; now it's their turn.)

●Choice of Friends

As Bette Midler sings, "You gotta have friends." And at no time in life is it more intense than in those formative teenage years. Friends provide role models. They inspire and they teach. They help aid the socialization process, as they ease the transition from leaving the nest to entering the adult world. They offer a sense of belonging.

But those are good friends. A poor peer choice can result in drug or alcohol abuse—or violence and worse. It can spiral a teen into a depression. So...although you don't want to pick your child's friends, it's important that you approve of them—and that he or she abides by this rule.

●Artistic, Creative, and Intellectual Endeavors

They say that youth is wasted on the young—and nowhere is this more obvious than in creative pursuits. Piano lessons, drawing, browsing through the paper...how many of us wouldn't welcome a few hours for these "luxuries?" On the other hand, how many of us balked, whined, and just plain hollered when our parents made us do them? But, thanks to the family contract, you can circumvent all the noise with a few specific rules. As proof that your child has practiced or read through some non-school-related literature, have him play a piece or have her summarize one or two articles she's read before assigning points. (Do keep in mind that your child doesn't have to be Chopin. Even an enthusiastic "Chopsticks" deserves at least one point—which will help reinforce positive feelings about the overall contract itself.)

The family contract aside, encouraging creative expression has an extra benefit for parents. It offers new insight into the emotional life of your child. Seeing what he draws. Hearing how she plays a musical instrument. Discussing his perceptions of the news. Now, that's what I call "quality time."

●Exercise

We all know the benefits of exercise—and, to make it a long-term daily habit. You can't start too young. Get your child into the groove with a few exercise rules: taking a walk, riding a bike, or dribbling a few balls in the local basketball court.

●Scheduled Extra Lessons

These are the unique "extras" that may or may not pertain to your teen. Special tutoring classes in algebra or geometry, band or majorette practice, extracurricular football or soccer after school, remedial reading, religious school and attending church or synagogue—all of these specific lessons should become rules that must be followed in order to receive extra points.

●Personal Hygiene

Let's start with hair. Try, if at all possible, to avoid any power struggles about your kid's hair unless the style is so outrageous, it's messing up your TV reception. Letting your child decide her own hairstyle (as long as it doesn't conflict with school regulations) may be one strategic way of "letting her win the battle so you can win the war." (For some reason I have never understood, hairstyles have provided more fertile battleground for parents and their offspring than just about any other issue—including drugs.)

Other rules governing appearance? Daily bathing, appropriate clothing, nutrition that includes at least something for each major food group. (That's milk, protein, bread, and fruit and vegetables—not Twinkies, soda, French fries, and deep-fried pork rinds.)

●Pet Care

This includes feeding, watering, walking, cleaning the litter box, and giving medication. (By doing these to your kids, they, in turn, learn how to care for Chubbuz the gerbil.)

●Medical Care

Weekly orthodontist appointments are important to keep—as are scheduled visits to the dentist, doctor, and therapist. And, if your child is recovering from alcohol or drug abuse, attending support group meetings is a criti-

---

CLAUSE PAUSE

Positive Peer Pressure

Kids coercing kids to try drugs. Smoke cigarettes. Cut school. We hear a lot about peer pressure in negative terms—so much so that we forget it can also be quite positive. It can go far in charging siblings up and keeping their energy high—the Group Award dangling before their eyes.

In fact, peer pressure is one of the most powerful shaping tools of adolescent behavior. It gets them to a point where they are embarrassed to be seen in public with their own parents. For several weeks I tried to figure out why my daughter was walking twenty yards ahead of us at the mall. Could it be my breath? My clothes? Something I said? Eventually, I decided not to take it personally. I realized that being seen with one's parents in the local mall is simply uncool. So I let her walk ahead. But, since she's only 13, I kept her in watching distance.

---

cal rule that must be kept. (See Chapter Nine on drug and alcohol abuse.)

●General Attitude and Behavior

Your teenager might practice piano. He might do all his homework. She might consistently be in bed with the lights out at the right time for a week. In fact, your child might do everything expected of him—but with a large amount of squawking, indecipherable feedback, sarcasm, and shadow-boxing. Thus, this final category. Not only will the completed chore itself get rewarded, but the *way* it's completed. Punctuality, respectful tone, good manners, and initiative—all deserve rewards in the form of points.

These, then, are the general rules that make up a

family contract. But seeing them listed in black and white doesn't mean they'll work for you. Let's face it. If your child already did all these things, you wouldn't have even opened this book. But, believe it or not, there's no magic wand, no abracadabra spell, that will get your child to follow these rules. But he or she will usually come around. Here's why:

The Point System

Each rule above is assigned a specific number of points—ranging anywhere from 0 to 5. (See how I assigned points in my sample contract.) When children complete a chore or follow a rule, they receive points for their efforts. The more points, the more privileges—which every child wants. On the other hand, the fewer points, the fewer privileges.

The lowest range on the point scale is always zero—which signifies virtual noncompliance with the rule. Think of zero as the mathematical equivalent of the equally useful "no"—and it should be applied even when the excuse is a creative and imaginative one.

The upper limit of the point score varies from rule to rule because some of them are simpler and more straightforward than others. For example, feeding the dog is pretty much an all or nothing proposition and, therefore, warrants a narrow point range of 0 to 1. Others, however, are more complex and open to subjective interpretation; these rules require a wider point range. For example, a well-made bed deserves some points, but neat sheets do not a neat room make. In the "Cleaning Your Room" category under "Routine Chores," you might want to give this one a range of 0–3.

Points should be tallied every day at the same time and place—as close to bedtime as possible. Your children should get points only for tasks completed before lights out. (We don't want them to go out at 11:30 PM to wash the car.)

Adding up the day's tallies is a job for both parents—but each of you will carry different weight in the different categories. Let's say your kids have been engaging in hand-to-hand combat with you all day long, only to clean up their act for the two hours they spent with Dad when he came home from work. It's only fair that Mom assigns the points for "General Attitude and Behavior" for that day.

When assigning points, you must also take into account not only the quality of the work itself, but the difficulty of the task. For instance, mowing the lawn with a hand mower takes more work than using a riding mower.

An especially high point rating might be reserved for infrequent events that represent much effort and work; these can be considered "bonus points." A good report card. A completed school science project. Charity work. Any of these deserve plaudits.

Similarly, you might want to give extra "weight" (more points) on particular problem areas that see improvement. If the arena for these problems is school, you might want to involve the school counselor or teacher in your plans. You can set up a system in which your child is responsible for bringing home a note from the teacher—who has assigned points to his behavior in class each day. (What makes this system especially good is the fact that it prevents the vicious cycle of the "I lost my note in the typhoon on the way home" syndrome; both you and your child know you only have to speak to his teacher to find out the day's points. Or better yet, if the typhoon ate his note, he gets 0 points in that category for that day.) If a babysitter watches your kids for a good number of hours each day, his or her input should be obtained as well.

Anything that approximates respect toward the teacher or babysitter can be assigned at least one point—so your child has something positive to show you. This way, too, you have an opportunity to give the child lots of "strokes" (I mean praise, not the belt) for that single point. Don't lay it on too thick, but you can say something like, "Wow, you're really improving. This is really a step in the right direction. I'm proud of you—and I'll bet you do even better in the future." Using this kind of encouragement sets a whole different tone from one in which teacher/sitter calls you at work to say, "Johnny's doing it again"—and you spend the next week in intense nightly arguments filled with predictions of doom and gloom if he doesn't "straighten out."

This encouragement is all part of that positive reinforcement I talked about in Chapter Three. (You probably recall. I described training a horse to turn left by feeding him a sugar cube.) It's also an example of "behavioral shaping"—which takes positive reinforcement one step further. With behavioral shaping, you'd give a sugar cube to the horse for any movement that is even vaguely leftward in direction—at least in the beginning. As the horse learns that leftward motion earns the sugar cube, a trainer will "up the stakes" and withhold the cube until he turns even further left. Through trial and error, the horse learns what earns sugar. Gradually, a complete leftward turn is "shaped"—and, what took many sugar cubes to learn, now requires only one.

In not too great a leap of the imagination from horses to typical adolescents, the points you assign in the family contract are the "sugar cubes." (I tried using actual sugar cubes with my kids but the dental bills became exorbitant.) By giving a task a wide point range, you're allowing these positive behavior-shaping techniques to take hold. For example, if your teen "cleans her room" for a grand total of 15 seconds, transforming it from the appearance of an Andes mountain mudslide to that of an Andes mountain mudslide with a partially made bed, the opportunity exists to award a point. And giving your daughter a single point out of a possible five for making that bed increases the likelihood that the room will gradually get cleaner over the coming weeks.

As you can see, points, like teens, can be complex. It's best to remember that your family contract will not be perfect from Day One. Assigning points is, in many ways, a study in trial and error. We had to reassign

CLAUSE PAUSE

Parents Don't Need Rules

In their attempt to denigrate your family contract, your kids will undoubtedly propose that it include rules for you to follow. Look at the sample contracts. There are no rules for parents anywhere to be found. The rules are just for kids. Period.

You might also point out that the rules only govern your kids' actions. They have nothing to do with your children's thoughts or feelings. That's because your kids are entitled to their opinions. However, you don't have to listen to them repeated hundreds of times.

several point values after trying out the contract for a few weeks. Here's a telling story:

Initially, we had assigned "washing the dishes" a point value of three—which was the same value we assigned to "exercising." When I asked my kids after dinner to do the dishes, they declined, retiring instead to the living room to perform a cross between Jane Fonda's Workout and professional wrestling, a discipline they termed "Exercising for Points." I was stuck doing the dishes and no one was giving me any points. I handled my frustration well by pretending to be Uri Geller and bending various kitchen utensils when no one was looking. But, when we ran out of silverware, Alyson and I both agreed that it was time to revamp the contract. We changed "exercising" to two points and gave "washing the dishes" five. With this simple adjustment, the two girls actually got into an argument over who would do the dishes one night; both of them insisted that they wanted to do the dishes alone so that they could get the entire five points. (That doesn't happen very often. In fact, it only happened twice, but whenever I examine my hands for signs of dishpan dermatitis, these memories spring to mind.)

In any event, through this process of trial and error, Alyson and I eventually found the right balance and relationship between point quantities and the different rules. Believe it or not, you too will find what works best for your individual family circle.

Leveling Off

Okay, you say. My child completes a task. In fact, she's washed the dishes and cleaned her room all week. All I have to do now is add up all her points and figure out the privileges she's earned.

Yes—and no. Points do determine privileges—but indirectly. If you assigned a different privilege for every, say, 10 points, your contract would become cumbersome (sort of like *Crime and Punishment* in the original Russian). It would be difficult to keep track of when, where, and what—for both you and your teen. To help keep things simple and organized, you need to add another step: Levels.

The family contract has four levels. (I recommend no more than four for efficiency's sake.) Each week, your child is assigned to one of them, based on the amount of points he or she earned. These levels determine the privileges your child will have for an entire week.

Like life, the higher the level, the more privileges— and vice versa. Level Four, as the highest, should include privileges that convey trust in your teen; they should be rewards, such as unlimited phone privileges, that you believe your child can handle with self-restraint and maturity.

And don't worry about your child's ability to handle this freedom. The beauty of this contract is the fact that self-restraint is built in. If a teen has achieved Level Four, she cannot interpret "unlimited" as her license to stay on the phone for hours. Why? Because she simply won't have time to do the necessary activities to keep her up there at that level. Fewer chores automatically means fewer points. And fewer points automatically means a drop in Level Privileges the following week—without you having to say a thing!

The lowest level, obviously, is One. It's equivalent to what many parents would term "grounding"—which varies tremendously from household to household. There's no allowance, no phone, no television, etc. But even though privileges are virtually nonexistent (except, of course, the "privilege" of boarding in your house), Level One's rewards should be spelled out as explicitly as the other three. After all, you are trying to teach something here—not punish.

Think of Level One as the optimist's half-filled glass as opposed to the pessimist's half-empty one. When your child drops down to Level One, he is not being "punished." He has, instead, lost a reward—and rewards are what the family contract is all about. Perhaps your kids get to watch TV one week because they've earned the privilege. But two weeks earlier, the TV was silent—not because they were bad, but because they *hadn't earned any viewing time.* A subtle difference, yes, but it keeps positive reinforcement strong.

Level assignments should be made once every week on the same day and at the same time. This routine helps incorporate the family contract into your life without hassle. (However, if your child is young, you might need to adjust this once a week rule. Younger children have less impulse control; their memory is less developed and they can lose momentum without more than once a week feedback.)

Assigning levels once a week also teaches both you and your teen a lot about life. Here's an illustration:

Say your child attained Level Four status—only to revert back to his obnoxious Level One behavior immediately after receiving his new privileges. According to the rules of the contract, he gets "his cake and eats it, too." He has an entire week to enjoy his freedom—and act like a Level One child. This, of course, can be very frustrating to you. But, like your son, you must wait and be patient. It helps to realize that a valuable lesson is being learned here: What we do and say one week can have profound ramifications for us the following week. (Actually, I prefer the Chinese philosophy that in life there are no rewards or punishments, only consequences.)

Here's another example, illustrating the opposite situation:

Let's say your child has dropped to Level One because of bad behavior that past week. She immediately cleans up her act in response to the loss of privileges—and earns a high Level Four point score. But she still has to ride out the week with Level One privileges. However, she does learn to wait for things that are important. And, because she knows that "acting out" will lower her point score and keep Level Four privileges out of reach, she also learns how to channel frustration and anger into more positive actions. (Incidentally, a child who learns frustration tolerance, good impulse control, and the need to earn what one wants will never grow up with the Borderline Personality or Narcissistic Character Disorders I discussed in Chapter Three.)

Privileges

At last. The golden ring. The prize. The "rocket fuel" that keeps your contract going strong. Without desirable privileges, the contract sits on the launching pad and is eventually towed away. And, without carefully selected and handled privileges, your contract won't fly.

First of all, you must be certain that you can provide the privileges. (There's nothing that will bring your contract to a grinding halt than promising, say, two tickets to a Madonna concert and not following through in delivering them when your child reaches the appropriate level.)

Secondly, you must be careful not to make the assumption that what you consider desirable is desirable to your child. Rewards such as a year's subscription to *The Wall Street Journal* or an all-you-can-eat evening at the local sushi bar might produce little excitement in the juvenile quarter. Such privileges might cause the child to work his way to Level One and stay there.

CLAUSE PAUSE

The Point of a Clean Room is Not Necessarily a Well-Made Bed

In perhaps the most hotly debated topic of the decade, second only to whether Jimmy Hoffa is really buried underneath the Giants Stadium, we encounter is the question, *"What is a clean room, anyway?"*

Despite recent scientific advances, the "clean room" continues to evade precise definition. There are those parents who are of the "Let Them Wallow in Their Own Underwear" philosophy. These are the parents who shoulder the kids' bedroom door closed as new quantities of unwashed stuff piles up from the center of the room outward. Then there are those who feel compelled periodically to locate their children within this pile to reassure themselves that the kid's vital signs are stable. These parents are in danger of succumbing to the compulsion to begin folding shirts and hauling baskets of laundry.

Don't despair. The family contract is here. If your child wants his points for cleaning his room, he's going to have to do it—before you get your cleaning compulsion and get there first.

It's simple. Only the child who cleans the room gets the points. This prevents our adolescents from entering the difficult arena of labor relations by attempting to hire migrant workers to come to the house to vacuum.

How do we determine what our kids really want? I give you the startling solution to this eternal dilemma: Ask them. Sometimes they will actually tell you. If you're lucky enough to get a straight answer from your child, see if you can simultaneously locate a piece of paper and a pencil with a point and write it down. Unfortunately, many parents won't write down their child's wish, but will instead attempt to persuade him that he is wishing for the wrong thing. "You really don't want the red cowboy hat, do you? The white one is so much nicer." If you find yourself trying to convince your kid that the white one is the right one, go ahead and get the white one for yourself. Then get him the one *he* wants.

Of course, a child's wish is not always your command. Kids will *always* choose privileges that are totally out of line first. (My daughters, for example, wanted a world tour of amusement parks in 18 cities.) They may request liberalizing their curfew time to, oh, 3:00 A.M. They may request a trip on the Concorde and back. They may request posters in the room of rock bands attempting to copulate with various stringed and keyboard instruments. For these and other outrageous requests, there's nothing like the unbelievably concise two letter word that starts with an "n" and ends with an "o."

More reasonable requests include the use of the television, the phone, and the family car—as well as upping an allowance. Another powerful reward can be unsupervised time with friends. (Notice that I said unsupervised—not unstructured. This way your teen is still responsible for telling you where he's going, when he's coming back, who he'll be with, and what he'll be doing. It also means you can ask him to "check in" with you during the night.)

One final note: Kids sometimes protest that the philosophy of the contract is to "bribe" them with privileges to comply with rules. Don't let them distort things with semantics. According to that logic, a paycheck for a good work week could also be considered a "bribe."

You've done it. You've spent the last few weeks compiling the rules, determining the points, and figuring out each level's privileges. But, despite your effort, your family contract could still lay the proverbial egg. In the same way you might rehearse before a big office presentation or take more pains with your appearance before an important lunch, so too must you put your best foot forward when it comes to the family contract. Here are some brief strategies to make yours a winner from Day One:

Brief #1: Editing

Every parent has a different opinion about what the house rules should be. This is America, where individualism is cherished nearly as much as Michael Jackson. The issue is not so much whether Johnny must be home by 9:00 or 9:30 on school nights, but whether Johnny gets the same message from Mom and Dad about his curfew. If he hears 9:00 from Dad and 9:30 from Mom, he's going to feel, at some level, that "If they can't even agree on something this simple, there's got to be a major problem here." This thought stirs anxiety. Unfortunately, kids aren't in the habit of tapping parents on the shoulder and informing them that they are nervous. Instead, they'll ignore the curfew altogether and walk in the front door at midnight.

To avoid this problem, make sure that your spouse has also reviewed and edited the contract. Until all parenting figures are in agreement with the contract's specifics, it should not be presented to the kids. If this negotiating process between the two of you takes months, it is still preferable to wait than to present a contract that only one parent will support. Trying to establish the contract prematurely is like trying to ride a bike with only one wheel. It can be done, but it turns into a real circus. (See Chapter Eight for more detail on the negotiating process between parents.)

Brief #2: Marketing

When you and your spouse have reached a consensus, it's time to type the contract. I suggest typing over handwriting not only for legibility, but to make the document itself appear as official-looking as possible. Parchment paper will add even more authenticity.

Putting the contract on a word processor is even better

than typing. Not only can you make revisions more easily, but, if you can obtain the software, you can change the typeface from ordinary pica to impressive large print or Old English (the kind with lots of cobwebs on the letters) styles. (See sample contracts.)

The main point here is that your contract should not be "user-friendly." It should look a little intimidating. Don't expect anyone to take you seriously if your contract is presented hand-scrawled on a supermarket bag.

Brief #3: Signing

Because we're striving for a serious tone here, it doesn't hurt to have your kids' names printed at the bottom of the contract with a space for their signatures. Signing their names helps establish a feeling of commitment and cooperation on their part. Besides, kids don't get to sign important-looking documents very often— which adds to overall feeling that you mean business.

Brief #4: Posting

When the contract is all typed up and the margins are straight, make one copy for each family member—plus one extra. This one's for the refrigerator door (where all other irreplaceable family documents are displayed). There, between the vacation photo of the kids shaking hands with Fred Flintstone and their drawing of a tyrannosaurus biting off the horn of triceratops, sits the family contract, suspended by the solitary Smurf-magnet. (This reminds me of an eerie incident that occurred one evening when I was home alone. While I was sitting at the kitchen table, the magnetic Smurf fell off the refrigerator— an apparent suicide. I try not to read too much into these things, though.)

For those of you without a refrigerator, simply nail the contract with railroad spikes through your child's bedroom door, Martin Luther style.

Brief #5: Announcing

A little ritualism can go a long way in establishing the family contract. When it is ready for presentation, don't just distribute copies over the meat loaf. For a real touch of importance, announce a family meeting at a given date and time.

Unfortunately, this can sometimes be easier said than done. In those families in which the contract has been long overdue, it might be difficult to get the kids to attend. I suggest you don't broach the subject of the meeting. Simply say, in as slow and somber a tone as possible, that a meeting has been scheduled and that the topic will be announced at the meeting itself. This makes some kids curious and can increase the likelihood of their showing up. (If things are so out of control that you can't even get the kids to show up or listen, it's time for professional help.)

Brief #6: Introducing

The night you have your first family contract meeting needs just the right environment, one that will set a precedent for the way future meetings will be conducted. If possible, arrange for your family to sit around a table that's about twenty feet long. For the serious factor, use straightback wooden chairs. Ceremonial feather pens are a nice touch and, after they're used for the signatures, they can be handed out as souvenirs.

Lighting, too, is important. Strap a flashlight around your chest and point it upward to create the "Boris Karloff effect." Proper attire can enhance this affect. British-style red judges' robes, complete with full wig, or, in a pinch, an ordinary tuxedo can go far in making this a real occasion.

Total silence is necessary when presenting the contract (unless you wish to add some color with "Hail to the Chief" playing immediately prior to your speech.) Once everyone is quiet, begin your introductory remarks—which is going to require a bit of a performance from both you and your spouse. (See Chapter Six for some hints on communicating with kids.) Come right to the point and tell them that the family contract is in effect as of today. Describe it in as simple language as possible. Use examples.

If you are inclined to give explanations to your kids (and they are inclined to listen without interruption), you might share with them the purpose and philosophy of the family contract. In case you need clarification:

1. The *purpose* is to reaffirm or reinstate parental control of the household and...
2. ...the *philosophy* embraces the concept that one cannot gain privileges in life without assuming corresponding responsibilities. Like poles on a magnet, you can't have one without the other.

Right after your introductory remarks, distribute copies of the contract. Or, better yet, fax it to the kids the day before the meeting. (Keep the original in a plastic explosives-proof box down at the bank.)

Brief #7: Anticipating Protest

Yes, I guarantee you will hear vehement protest (or studied, casual disregard). Some of the protests might include statements like, "You're treating me like a kid." Be armed with this double-barreled reply: "Yes, that captures the spirit of the family contract very precisely. We *are* treating you like the kids and ourselves like the parents."

To avoid all-night arguments and tears, you may elect to open up the discussion—*but only for a limited time.* (Otherwise the question-and-answer period could exceed the length of *War and Remembrance.*) This open discussion may include the following:

q: When does it start?
a: Now.
q: Are you serious about this?
a: Yes.
q: Do we really have to do this?

A: Yes.

If your kids perceive that the contract is for real and that you are quite serious about it, they will stop trying to persuade you to abandon the whole project. Instead, they will begin negotiating the specifics—something like this:

Q: How come we only get ten minutes of phone privileges on Level Three?
A: Your mother and I spent a lot of time thinking through every element in this contract including that one.

And, always, expect the inevitable:

Q: Nobody else has to have contracts like this. How come we do?
A: Your mother and I have decided that this family contract is worth a try for our family. What other families do or don't do is none of our business.

Be prepared, too, for a possible power struggle immediately following your announcement. That's exactly what happened in my home. My daughters both informed me rather matter-of-factly that although the contract certainly looked like a nice piece of paper, they had no intention of following it. When they finished, I pointed out to them that if they did not follow the rules, they would get zeros in each category every day. And, when points were tallied at the end of the week, they'd be on Level One.

To hone in on the gravity of this situation, my wife and I then read out loud the list of Level One privileges. In a face-saving gesture, my daughters replied in unison, "I don't care." (However, as I noted earlier in the Introduction, my kids actually earned one of their all-time high point scores on the first day of the contract.)

Above all, remember that you do not owe your kids any explanation. If you are convinced in your own mind that the family contract is worthwhile and deserving of a trial period, that's all you need. Also keep in mind that your kids aren't really interested in explanations anyway—even though they say they are. What they are really interested in is talking you out of the whole idea.

Brief #9: Totaling Scores

I know. Adding up point totals every night sounds like a lengthy and laborious ordeal. And, quite frankly, it is—but only at first. As with most things, the more it is practiced, the smoother and faster it goes. Now that the family contract has been in place in our home for over a year, it usually takes only ten minutes to go down the checklist before bedtime. We have done this so many times that the kids have it memorized, anyway.

Some degree of ritualism or theatrics in the weekly point totaling and level assigning helps keep enthusiasm high. A nice visual aid, especially for younger children, is color-coded marbles representing points. By watching his colored marbles accumulate in a clear glass container, your child can measure his progress through the week. When we were using marbles, the Sunday count to determine levels for that week provided some very dramatic moments—and even fun.

Read your child's new level privileges out loud. Congratulate her on a job well done—or boost up her confidence for the lower level week ahead. Count out your child's allowance for the week—and give it to him at this time. Drama makes for entertainment that will, in turn, make your child stay tuned in for the week ahead.

Brief #10: Adding Group Rewards

Once your contract is up and running (or at least walking), you may want to consider adding an extra feature. Although there's a lot to be said for keeping things simple, variation can add zest—and keep enthusiasm high.

The contract as I have presented it is really capitalism in its purest form. It is individualized to each child so

that one sibling can be on Level Four and another on
Level One at the same time. But some parents might be
concerned that this situation will raise adults who are
"only out for themselves."

For those concerned parents out there, I offer a solid
solution: the Group Reward System. This provision offers
a very special prize to all your kids if they are all at a
high level in the same week.

But high doesn't necessarily mean Level Four. Trying
to attain Level Four status to receive an award can
foster some bad habits:

One of your children might be making such a high
point score that she surpasses even Level Four—while,
at the same time, her sibling might still be on Level
One. The high scorer might end up playing the role of
rescuer—doing some of brother's chores for him—so they
can win the group prize. The low scorer, in turn, can
learn bad dependency habits.

To prevent this situation, don't choose Level Four as
the common level. Choose a lower level (Two or Three)
that all the kids can achieve without inhuman struggle.
This way, a climate is encouraged where the low man on
the totem pole gets support to raise his own points—
rather than riding on the family star's coattails.

By introducing this Group Award concept, you can
observe such incredible events as seeing one of your kids
actually helping another kid make his bed—both of
them accidentally discovering that chores really do go
faster when you work together.

Congratulations! You now have all the tools you need
to create a family contract. But, like all documents, it's
just a piece of paper—unless it's enforced. So before you
go ahead and sharpen that pencil, read on—and discover
the dynamics that will make your Contract soar.

CHAPTER FIVE

Loopholes, Revisions, and Enforcement

Picture this scenario: The dimmer switch for the dining room chandelier is on low. The table has been cleared. All that's left on its shiny wood surface are some serving platters of fruit and cookies. Your family sits around the dining room table. Your spouse is sipping coffee. Your three kids are waiting to bolt. There is an air of expectancy. You have just introduced the family contract; copies have been passed out to everyone. You are currently listening to the gasps and inhuman groans coming from your kids....

That's okay. You've read this book and nothing they are saying is taking you by surprise. You expected protest; you're holding firm. But wait...what's this? Your kids run out of the room. They're screaming: "No way we're gonna do this. No way. And you can't force us. Forget about it."

By the end of the week, there were no clean rooms, no completed homework, no "lights out" honored. In short, none of your kids had made enough points to get out of Level One...

Unfortunately, many kids will actually go on strike as their first test of wills. They will indeed have insufficient points at the end of that first week to make Level One and parents are immediately thrust into the challenge of enforcing the contract.

And this and many other challenges will come. You can count on it. No matter how well thought out and specific your family contract may be, your kids will find approximately the same number of loopholes that Marvin Mitchelson might find in the Tyson-Givens prenuptial agreement. Don't worry if you can't find them in the first draft, because your kids will quickly point them out to you. That is their job. When they find a loophole, revisions in the contract may be necessary. In other situations, your child may find what he thinks is a loophole, but you may decide to simply interpret the existing rule without altering it.

But no matter the number of loopholes, the hours spent on revisions, or the countless discussions with your spouse, the bottom line will always be enforcement. Without proper enforcement, your family contract will never work.

Firmness and consistency are both important—as is flexibility. But kids can see past a stance that's faked or shaky. In order to be truly consistent, firm, and wise, you need to know exactly what you are doing—and why. You need to understand some of the dynamics that go into enforcement. They're all about the parent-child relationship—and how it is tested, pulled, pushed, and continually developed.

"LOVE ME, LEAVE ME ALONE", OR THE PULL OF DEPENDENCY VS. THE PUSH TOWARD INDEPENDENCE

Human beings are more dependent on their parents during infancy and childhood than any other species. A newborn colt is up and walking a few minutes after birth. So is a newborn bird. Or a lizard. Or a whale. Think of Mama Shamu, a whale at San Antonio's Sea World, who gave birth to a calf on live television. Immediately after birth, the baby began swimming and playing to the underwater camera. (I understand that Baby Shamu now has his own agent and is negotiating terms for his first Pepsi commercial.)

We humans, of course, are different. We come into this world in a totally helpless condition. So typical. Without continuous care and attention by parents, we do not survive. And necessary care transcends just food and shelter. In the 1940s, French researcher Renee Spitz proved that physical contact with the baby is a crucial aspect of parenting. He studied hospital nurseries where, to "prevent infections," nurses were instructed to touch the newborns as little as possible and to wear white gowns, masks and gloves. Over half the infants died; snuggling is apparently life-saving.

But dependence is only half the story. At the same time a child is clinging to her parents, she's also feeling the need to separate and find her own identity or, as child psychiatrists like to call it, "individuate." This separate process begins simultaneously with the need to bond. Thus, a child is caught in a double bind almost from Day One. In fact, this push towards independence versus the pull of dependence continues through adolescence. (Indeed, even as adults, we sometimes feel this push/pull.)

The contradictory needs both to separate and to belong are usually behind your teen's rebellious behavior. This inner conflict can create problems within the family contract as well.

Take Jean. She wanted to be out with her friends; she didn't want to spend time at home at all. When she looked at the family contract her mother and father so carefully constructed, she was appalled. How could they stop her from seeing her friends—or going to a party Saturday night! But this desire for independence clashed with the need she had for her parents to love her. She wanted the friends and the party—but, though she'd never admit it to her friends for fear of being called a "baby," she felt safer and strangely comforted with a curfew.

What's nice about a family contract is that it works on both needs. It takes care of Jean's need for independence by offering it as a privilege for a job well done. (Talk about motivation!) But it also takes care of the pull

---

CLAUSE PAUSE

Differentiation Dilemma

In the Academy Award-winning movie *Ordinary People*, the son announces to his family that he's quit the swim team. After he'd witnessed his brother's death by drowning, swimming had become fraught with too much pain and distress. Unfortunately, his mother reacts as if the decision were a personal attack on her. His coach also reacts angrily; he tries to pressure him to stay on the team. The implicit message from both his mom and his coach is that if he quits swimming, it is the beginning of the end of his whole life. But, in reality, it is probably the healthiest thing he could do...

---

toward dependency and parental security by establishing specific boundaries and consistent rules.

Margaret Mahler, one of the pioneers in separation and individuation, divided the process into gradual stages. Here, very briefly, are a few of the events that signal these different stages:

●Refueling

Notice a toddler during a typical day and you'll see him literally run away from his parents—over and over again. He doesn't much care what direction he's running in, as long as it is "away" from Mom and Dad. When the child runs away in a safe, baby-proof environment, a parent can stay put, seizing the opportunity to get past page one of the newspaper for the first time in months. But before a parent finishes the first headline, the child's back—insisting to be picked up and held. This is how the child is "refueled" with parental affection, attention, and physical contact. When he's "filled up," it is

time to squirm and be put down—so he can run off
again.

This process continues until the duration between
refueling periods is long enough for the child to be able
to sit through an entire episode of *Sesame Street*. This
roughly correlates to the point where Dad is able to
make it all the way through the sports section. (However, kids generally do not want you looking at a newspaper when you could be looking at them. This message is
subtly conveyed when they rip the paper from your
hands and instantly convert it to an impressively large
spitball.)

●Narcissism

It's a typical scene. Parents, in-laws, grandparents,
friends, and neighbors pick up an infant and begin
speaking to her in the traditional Minnie Mouse voice.
Everything about her is "sooooo cuuuute." She is told
repeatedly that she has the cutest toes, the cutest nose,
the prettiest smile, the softest skin, the most this, the
biggest that, and the tiniest other thing. We all need a
good whopping dose of this drivel so that we develop
some level of self-esteem and self-worth. (Freud described the infant's role in the family as "King Baby.")

But as the child separates from her parents and begins to explore the world around her, she begins to
realize some limits on her grandiose self-perception. For
one, she encounters other children who are just as, if not
more, narcissistic and grandiose as herself. Their mutual senses of entitlement conflict in a struggle over a
Strawberry Shortcake doll. The child is confused, angry
and helpless as the doll is wrested away from her 2-year-old
grasp by one of those hulking, greedy 4-year-olds. She
articulately expresses these feelings with a scream more
destructive than Ella Fitzgerald's Memorex voice. (Such
cries from my own children have occasionally warped my
contact lenses, blurring the entire visual field.) Yes, she
is learning to make her way into the world.

●Testing Limits

We've all experienced this. When you tell a small child not to touch the television, he will immediately walk up to the screen and put his hand approximately a quarter inch from its surface. He will then attempt to establish eye contact with you to make sure you're watching his every move. What does this have to do with separation and individuation? Plenty. By waddling over to the television, your child is telling you in the only language he knows that he is a separate entity. But by looking back at you, he's also saying that he still needs external control to manage his impulses. If your child was unable to make eye contact with you, chances are he would have touched the screen. This, too, says something: What happens when I break the rules? If you continue to be unresponsive, he probably will pick up the decorative paperweight from the coffee table and knuckleball it right at Oprah.

He's still testing you when, years later, he comes home at 10:05 PM instead of 10:00 PM on his first night out with the car. Some parents might not even notice he was five minutes late. Still others might choose to ignore it. Still others may try to explain why it's important for him to follow the rules, an exercise that has everyone up all night. But the smart parents are the ones who simply enforce the rule.

Even if it's maladaptive, annoying, and self-destructive, it's important to remember that "testing limits" is your child's way of forming a separate identity from Mom and Dad. If you regard this behavior as part of your child's natural growth, you won't see it as a personal vendetta— and you'll be able to enforce the contract rules with more objectivity and fairness.

●Togetherness

We've all seen the families whose every member wears identical Hawaiian shirts, those close-knit folks who go skating, to the movies, to Disney World and back *together*. In fact, Mom and Dad believe so strongly in "togetherness" that the day their child decides she doesn't want to go bowling becomes fraught with crisis. Interrogation soon follows while her parents try to find out what's "wrong" with her.

The truth is that there's nothing wrong with her. She simply discovered that she doesn't like bowling. What's "wrong" with this situation is her parents' attempt to make her seem like she is in the wrong. This, as many of you might find familiar, is called a "guilt trip." As one adolescent girl described it: "Guilt is the gift that keeps on giving." The trouble with guilt is that:

1. Pressure to go bowling can backfire—and send the girl even further away from her parents or...
2. She'll don the Hawaiian shirt and go bowling with the family. Her parents are no longer angry and depressed—but she is.

Well-known family therapist Dr. Murray Bowen coined the term "differentiation" for this variation on the separation-individuation theme. Dr. Bowen believed that differences in personal taste and talents between family members are not only acceptable, but should be encouraged. When healthy differentiation is allowed, the separation-individuation process can advance with the family contract rules intact. Your son can demonstrate that he's different than you by choosing to play basketball with his friends as one of this week's privileges instead of going skating with you. Clearly, this is a much more positive way of establishing independence than testing his limits on his curfew.

Of course, it's important for the family to be together on occasion. In fact, some activities should be for family members only—with no guests allowed. I recommended this as a nonnegotiable rule so that these "family only" events take place on a regular basis. In the same vein, I also feel a child needs encouragement to continue certain hobbies or lessons—even if he seems resistant. Because the family contract offers points for practice, your child has a built-in inducement. But you must use your judgment here. When encouragement on your part becomes coercion through the use of sarcasm, hostile criticism, and/or guilt, your child will probably give up playing piano altogether for his new hobby—vandalizing missile silos.

RISKY BUSINESS, OR, MAKING MISTAKES

No one likes to be wrong—especially kids. In fact, when presented with the option of making their own choices, kids will often balk. What if they make a mistake? I remember standing in a convenience store waiting for my daughter to decide what type of soda to buy; she wanted me to make the decision for her. I told her that I would not—and if she didn't decide within the next two minutes, we'd leave the store without any soda at all. This is certainly an innocuous example, but for my daughter, it was good practice for taking risks, making decisions, and accepting the fact that mistakes really are all right as long as we learn from them.

As this example shows, mistakes can be useful. In certain Japanese corporations, executives are required to make a yearly quota of mistakes. No mistakes means no action and no work. As Billy Joel sings in his song "Second Wind," "You're supposed to make mistakes." (Incidentally, this song is an autobiographical piece inspired by his adolescent experience with depression and suicidal thoughts.)

The family contract is a good vehicle for your child to learn the "art" of mistakes. He learns that if he makes the mistake of breaking a rule, he'll drop to a lower level—and he'll have to accept the consequences of his actions. By earning approval and privileges for a job well done, she learns to have more confidence in herself—a fertile climate for positive risk-taking.

CLAUSE PAUSE

A Good Night's Sleep

Kids hate to go to bed. They will generally become more "hyper" as bedtime approaches, commencing a triatholon in the living room about five minutes before bedtime. They frequently want to wrestle with you into the night. Even after reading the entire life works of Big Bird together, your child will want yet another bedtime story. He will give you a goodnight hug around the neck which feels good for the first five minutes, but then begins to feel a lot like the ancient Manchurian Everlasting Grip of Death. Attempting to pry those little fingers off your carotid arteries gets difficult as circulation to the head and neck region is compromised. The larynx is simultaneously compressed, making calling out for help an impossibility...

Why do kids hate to go to sleep so much? I remind you of the famous picture of the Harlow monkey from your high school biology class. You remember. It's the one showing this scared little baby monkey hanging on to a cloth-covered wire cage that the baby thinks is "Mom." (We may have just stumbled onto the solution to the babysitter shortage crisis.) Sleep is, after all, a form of separation. In the child's mind, a separation is a separation— whether it is going out for the evening, divorce, death, or going to bed. Hopefully, they eventually see the distinctions, but in the meantime, you have finger marks deep in the neck region.

One possible solution is to approach the separation issue gradually. To do this, you must resign yourself to sleep deprivation for at least a few nights. However, this might be viewed as a short-term investment for long-term gain. When your child begins to protest and cry as you leave his room, tell him that you'll return in five minutes. (For a younger child who has no idea what "five minutes" means, tell him to say the alphabet five times *slowly* and you'll be back.) Above all, make sure you return in five minutes. If you're lucky, your kid will be asleep, but probably not. Repeat the process, this time saying you'll return in ten minutes. . . .

You might need to continue this process for a few hours at first, but, as the nights go by, it will become a less lengthy process. If not, it might be time to seek professional help.

YOU SAY "POTATO," I SAY "POTAHTOE," OR, AGREE TO DISAGREE

When your kids complain about the rules in your weekly family meeting, don't worry about getting the last word. The last word is the family contract. You can simply agree to disagree—while reminding your children that the rules of the contract are still in force. Voicing one's disagreement is healthy; it promotes independence and individuality; it offers a chance to take a risk.

Unfortunately, your children can easily disagree all night long. It's best to put a limit on the time you spend hearing disagreements and protests; it shouldn't take up the whole weekly meeting. But the time you do allot should have your undivided attention.

You might also want to point out that complaints will be more likely to result in actual change if they are accompanied by proposed solutions. By agreeing to disagree, you're not only encouraging your kids to have their own opinions, but you're also teaching them to look for solutions and solve problems—which will help them much more in life than whining or acting out.

"YOU DON'T TRUST ME," OR, PROTESTING IN BLACK AND WHITE

People might trust me to drive their car, but they shouldn't trust me to fly their plane since my piloting experience is limited to flying a remote control P-38 in my high school parking lot. In fact, their "lack of trust" in my flying ability is realistic and necessary for everyone's survival. Similarly, you may trust your child on Level Two to go outside to play and return home before dark. But you shouldn't trust his judgment and impulse control enough to allow him to stay out until 10:00.

The fact is that trust is not black or white. Unfortunately, when you're a child, it's a difficult concept to understand. Like the Borderline adult, children either trust someone—or they don't. Unfortunately, that simplistic view of trust is usually hurled in your face (usually when you're driving your trusty car in a freeway traffic jam). "You don't trust me!" is a common family contract protest among kids.

But don't let it throw you. You owe no explanation to your kids, nor do you have to get defensive when they begin to protest. And do keep in mind that the kids who demand "reasons" are the same ones who will skeet-shoot your explanations as soon as they are launched.

"I LOVE GRANDMA AND GRANDPA MORE THAN YOU," OR, STOPPING GRANDPARENT GENEROSITY

There's nothing like a doting grandparent—unless he or she is undermining your family contract. The relationship between grandchild and grandparent is entirely different than the complicated one you share with your child. Grandparents don't have to discipline. They don't have to listen to the shouts. They don't have to raise your kid. They already raised one; they can go home.

A case in point is when a "generous" grandparent gives his grandchild money without your permission.

You approach Grandpa, attempting to explain the concept of behavioral modification to him. You eloquently explain how important it is to tightly regulate rewards so that they are given only for desirable behavior. You offer to lend him your copy of this book so he can understand and participate in the family contract. Then, sadly, you learn that Grandpa has turned off his hearing aid for the afternoon as he replies, "Behoovioral whoosit?" Worse yet, Grandpa rejects the whole idea as a "bunch of malarky... All I did was give the kid a little money for a pellet gun. What's the big deal?"

Grandparent abuse carries roughly the same penalties as child abuse in most states, so forget it. Instead, think of Grandpa as a loophole in the contract that can be fixed. You simply instruct your teen that he can't accept gifts or money from anyone without parental permission. Like all rules in the contract, it will be up to him to be honest and report such "gifts" to you. And, like the other rules as well, if this one is broken, the secret will eventually come to light. (Don't forget: Some grandparents like to test limits, too.)

Enforcement is not only a matter of understanding the dynamics of the parent-child relationship. It's also a matter of....

LISTENING, PLUGGING UP LOOPHOLES, AND REVISING WHEN THE NEED ARISES

Now that you're armed with all this terrific psychological expertise, let's go to a specific example. Your adolescent son returns home at 9:05 PM for the 9:00 PM curfew. Aware as you are that he is "testing limits" and that it is important to confront this type of behavior early on, you assume your most authoritative pose and deepest voice to inform him that he gets a zero on this rule for the day—even though he's only five minutes late.

Your son responds that his watch says two minutes *before* nine. He points out, quite accurately, that the written contract did not specify whose watch would be

---

CLAUSE PAUSE

Sick Leave

How do you score points when your child is ill? This is a tough one because it's hard even for physicians to always discern genuine medical illness from psychosomatic complaints. As a rule of thumb, doctor-diagnosed problems should, of course, excuse your child from her chores. These include diarrhea, vomiting, or fever—as opposed to such purely subjective physical complaints as, "I'm not feeling well. My head hurts. I have a stomachache." If a physician finds no evidence of a physical problem, these complaints get no special treatment; continuing to excuse your child due to vague aches and pains only reinforces more of them.

---

used in determining the correct time for curfew. He further claims that his watch is more accurate than yours because he has a digital quartz chronometer and all you've got is Mickey's big hand on the five. So . . . you're being "unfair."

You've heard enough. You're ready to amend the contract to include specifics on whose watch should be used for keeping time. As tempting as it is, don't do it. Utilizing parental authority will work even better. Simply remind your son that in cases where loopholes exist and rules require interpretation, it is the *parents'* interpretation of the rules that stands. And, in this case, it means that you, as the parent, are the official timekeeper. (Since the parental role is already implied in each of the contract's rules, there's no need to amend or revise the contract. This also keeps things simple. By repeatedly invoking parental authority to interpret rules, you can keep from adding so many amendments to the family contract that it approaches the length of *War and Peace*.)

Parental authority notwithstanding, there will be times when there is a legitimate need for revisions. Your child's growth is such a legitimate need. A very young child will have very different rules and privileges from her teenaged sister. But, as she grows, her needs will change—and her rules and privileges must keep apace.

Revisions will also be required if there are any major loopholes that were overlooked in your first draft. Don't be discouraged at the amount of loopholes your kids find. Remember, just as kids are destined to test limits due to a gene located on Chromosome 5, Row 6, Seat 4, they are also destined to search relentlessly for loopholes in the contract.

The message to your children's proposed revision might be a categorical "no" or a "shoot from the hip yes" in which it is given a trial period to see how it works. Or you both might choose to deliberate, telling your kids that their idea deserves serious consideration and you will announce your final decision at next week's family meeting. The rule, until then, should stand as is—despite your kids' groans that they can't wait that long.

Whichever way you decide to handle revisions, it must be presented as a joint parental decision—with neither parent the villain. (This way you can both be "bad guys.")

Whether enforcing, revising or discussing loopholes, you won't get further than "Let's call this meeting to order" if you can't communicate with your kids. Read on....

CHAPTER SIX

Communicating with Kids

At a recent meeting with a local parents' group, I was asked how I would handle the following problem:

It seemed that one of the mothers was "unable to communicate" with her son, whom I shall call Mark. She described him as an intellectually gifted young man, especially in the sciences. But Mark was often so involved in astronomy and such that his "head was in the clouds" and he often didn't hear his mom when she talked. One day, while he was walking around the house, Mark absentmindedly dropped a towel on the kitchen floor. His mother told him to pick it up. He kept walking, presumably contemplating the atmospheric temperature of Venus. "Pick up the towel, Mark," Mom called out. But by then he was long gone....

I drew upon years of Freudian psychoanalytic training to come up with the solution to this one. I suggested a body block. Sure, Mark was a bit taller than Mom, but if she headed him off at the kitchen door quickly enough to get sure footing, she could lean a shoulder into his upper chest and stop him cold. That would certainly bring him back to planet earth and the realm of dropped towels.

Frankly, when it comes to communicating with kids, there's too much talk about "relating" and not enough about body blocks. In fact, the countless how-to parent books are loaded with words like relating and other psychobabble. If any of these books were discussing how to change a light bulb, it might read as follows:

When the individual encounters an area of darkness in his life he must gaze into the fifth plane of consciousness to assess his own level of codependency on the source of his affliction. It is only then that he can enter a more positive realm, bringing to bear the solution already within his environment, the light bulb. It will illuminate his kitchen with new meaning, new spirit, and a warm fuzzy of peaceful karma.

Pretty nauseating, yes? Besides, you still haven't been told how to put in the stupid bulb.

Obviously, communication is more than words. And it most definitely involves more than the latest fads and trends in the arena of child and adolescent psychiatry would have you believe. Over the past ten years, there has been a parade of pompous pop psychology explain-all approaches, such as:

- **Hyperactivity.** The kid moved again. Time for Ritalin.
- **The Feingold Diet.** Let's talk about how many red M & M's you ate today, okay?
- **Food allergies.** After being tested to 418 possible allergens and testing positive to 411, we learn the only safe place for the kid is Antarctica.
- **Megavitamins.** Now known to cause kidney stones and liver disease, but still available at the mall right next to the House of Cashews.
- **The Scared Straight approach.** If your kid gets caught stealing a Polo shirt, send him to death row for the weekend.
- **"Masked" depression.** Beware the telltale sign of uncontrollable giggling.
- **Hypoglycemia.** Have you had your glucose tolerance test today?
- **Just say no.** Nancy is so life-like.
- **Eating disorders.** Prevalence is now known to be only 1.5 percent among college-age women as opposed to the 50 percent statistics found in earlier reports. This new figure has resulted in the closing

down of approximately three million eating disorder programs in the greater Houston area alone.

- **Codependency.** A potentially useful concept, but someone has apparently reinvented the wheel because the notion of "dependency" has been around for a long time. Put a "co" in front of the word and its trendiness makes it the all-new, all-purpose diagnosis for anyone who has ever been nice to their spouse for anything whatsoever.
- **EST.** When you find *it,* you can use *it* for a while. Just make sure you put *it* back where you found *it.*
- **Dianetics.** The Cordon Bleu of Babble, this one's widely credited for single-handedly creating an entirely new psychobabble dialect.
- **Neurolinguistic programming.** I first heard about this one from a guy next to me on the plane. Next time I'm wearing the headphones for the entire trip, even if they're playing the Beastie Boys' Greatest Hits.

Believe it or not, there is a common thread to these and other psychology fads. All of them enjoy explosive growth and tend to last about a year. People are "diagnosed" by a checklist of symptoms so vague and exhaustive you'd have to be either comatose or from Duluth not to qualify. When enough items on the list are checked, the (aha!) "diagnosis" is reached. It turns out that all the kid's problems are explainable by one simple and long-overlooked solution. Bad school grades. A fight with his best friend. Good old depression. Social isolation. Drug use … all are due to the red dye #2 in his food. Remove the red dye from his diet and all his problems will miraculously disappear. (Parents have actually reported this and they will give sworn testimony that it works.)

It is my contention that the reason many of these fads work—at least temporarily—is that they provide a means of *communication between parent and child.* Think of it. If communication can work that well for megavitamins and neurolinguistic programming, imagine what it will do for your family contract!

CLAUSE PAUSE

Selective Hearing Deficit

With kids, Selective Hearing Deficit (SHD) is a source of incomparable parental misery. What's SHD? Here's an example:

Five progressively louder repetitions of the cogent and time-honored parent's motto, "Please take your seriously odor-impacted sweatsocks off the kitchen table" are met with dead silence and no observable movement whatsoever. Seconds later, the phone rings and this seemingly deceased being springs to life to sprint past us, reaching speeds previously thought achievable only in the superconductor supercollider.

Basically, communication is all about getting somebody's attention. If you are a parent, this somebody is usually your son or daughter. Yelling sometimes works, but it's kind of tough on the vocal cords and it can be downright embarrassing at the supermarket. Repetition also has undeserved popularity as an attention-getting technique. ("I tell him over and over again to pick up the towel and he just ignores me.")

But don't despair. There are some effective ways to get your child's attention before you have to resort to a body block. Let's go over these lines of communication now:

Line of Communication #1: Setting the Scene

Above all else, decide on a good time to have your talk with your teen. Planning ahead insures that you won't be explaining the meaning of life to him as you run out the door on your way to work. Once you do manage to find a ten-minute time slot between dropping off the dry cleaning and picking up your other kid from school, give him some advance notice of the upcoming summit conference. This way he can rearrange his schedule, too.

When the momentous time arrives, turn on the telephone answering machine, turn off the TV, and carefully lift the Walkman earphones from his head. Remove his sunglasses to establish good eye contact. Tell his friends to leave the house and wait for him at their favorite Stop 'N Go. Close the door and tell him to sit down. You sit down, too. Sitting down lends a nice civilized touch.

All set? Good. Now tell him to pick up his towels.

Line of Communication #2: Ignoring the Why

I would not advise you to ask your teen why he doesn't pick up his towels. You won't like the answer—which, more times than not, will be a variation of the safe, time-honored "I don't know." When you ask children why they do the things they do, they usually say, "I don't know." They say "I don't know" because they really don't know.

Further, it has never been very clear to me what a parent expects to hear when she asks her child why he doesn't pick up the towels. Who cares, anyway? We just want the towels picked up, that's all. (As famed existentialist philosopher, Pee Wee Herman puts it, "There are some things you shouldn't understand.")

Line of Communication #3: Keeping on Track

Be specific about your rules—and why you wanted to have this discussion in the first place. If you deliver a thirty-minute lecture on "responsibility," "relating," "communication," "respect," and "starvation in Ethiopia" without mentioning the towels, don't be surprised if you find them on the floor later that afternoon.

Staying focused on the subject at hand is easier if you talk slowly and don't raise your voice. Avoid using big words as well as these two small ones: "always" and "never." Like asking "why?" using these words are a sure-fire way to keep the safe, secure, and closed-minded "I don't know" alive.

Line of Communication #4: Fitting in Praise

Try to spend as much time praising as you do criticizing. Search your recent memory for something he has done well. Tell him you felt proud and happy the other day when he took out the trash without being asked. It showed that he understands what responsibility is. As a matter of fact, right now you're simply reminding him that you know he can show enough responsibility to pick up his towels, too.

Line of Communication #5: Avoiding Explanations

Explanations are not always feasible or desirable when dealing with kids—even when it's their turn to ask "why?" In fact, when kids ask you "why?" they don't actually want to know "why" the rule under discussion exists. What they're really asking is whether they have to follow the rule and what will happen if they don't.

When your child was 3 and refused to take a bath, you, the confident parent, simply picked him up and put him in the tub. An incompetent parent, however, would have tried to explain how being dirty could lead to bacterial growth on the skin, resulting in various infectious diseases, etc. This lecture would go on at length as Mom and Dad made use of their college microbiology course to explain to their toddler the difference between gram-positive and gram-negative anaerobic endocarditis. Meanwhile, there's no bath. . . .

Remember that "explanations" are not a part of the family contract. You know them and that should be good enough. Besides, your explanation could very well be beyond your child's capabilities. Children do have difficulty understanding symbolism, metaphor, and analogy; they are not yet developed sufficiently. For example, if you ask a child to interpret the proverb "People in glass houses shouldn't throw stones," he is likely to say, "Because it would break the glass."

Another telling example comes from a conversation I had with my younger daughter. I had asked her if she knew who George Bush's running mate was. She guessed it was his dog. I suddenly realized she thought "running mate" literally meant someone to jog with. In retrospect, however, Bush might have done better had he listened to her.

Line of Communication #6: Understanding Your Limits

Verbal communication doesn't mean self-righteous speeches about what your child should feel. The contract rules only deal with behavior. As I discussed in Chapter Five, there are absolutely no rules about your child's thoughts or emotions. They can *think* that cleaning their room is "stupid." They can *feel* angry about having that particular rule in the contract. It's okay. No matter. The rule stays in. End of talk.

But do keep in mind, however, that there are certain anger-based behaviors that are not allowed in the contract or in any discussions about the contract. Yelling, cursing, door slamming, procrastinating, and open refusal are not acceptable—and cost valuable points.

Line of Communication #7: Changing the Subject

Distraction can be a very powerful parenting technique. I remember learning a good distraction trick from my dad when my older daughter was about 3. She would sometimes awake from her nap in a cranky mood, and being a naive young father, I would try to figure out what was making her cry. In retrospect, I realize that she was still in the process of waking up and, like many of us, she was feeling irritable in those first few moments. My attempts to ask her what was wrong seemed to make her even more upset. Well, one day I was riding in the car with my father and daughter. She was asleep in his lap. When she awoke, she began her crying routine. But my dad immediately drew her attention to a button on her coat and asked her to button it. She stopped crying instantly and started telling him everything you could possibly want to know about buttons as

---

CLAUSE PAUSE

A Communication Lesson

A videotape produced by renowned family therapist Jay Haley shows the therapist in a session with a family troubled by a teenager's out-of-control behavior and a mother's depression:

The therapist asked Mom a question. The oldest daughter, who had taken it upon herself to "fill in" for her depressed Mom, jumped in to answer. As the daughter rambled on about her theories on her family's problems, Mom slunk further and further down in her chair.

At this point, the therapist intervened. He interrupted the daughter without even acknowledging that he had—and directed another question to Mom. His eye contact and body language were clearly aimed at Mom as well. The daughter now looked confused while Mom literally rose to the occasion. She sat upright and began to answer the therapist's question....

The power of this maneuver lay not so much in what the therapist did, but what he didn't do. Rather than focusing on *what* people were saying, he addressed the *way* things were being said. Through his intervention, he encouraged this mother to be a mom—not with words of advice she was too depressed to hear, but by treating her as if she already had the ability to fill this role.

---

well as an overview of the buttoning process itself. Anyway, it was much more preferable to the crying....

When a specific problem needs to be addressed, distraction only postpones the inevitable. But, as a way of circumventing all-night fights, tantrums, or crying jags, distraction can come in handy.

Line of Communication #8: Realizing Your Teen is Different From You and Me

Kids do struggle to understand the complexities of life. During infancy, they begin to perceive people as "good" or "bad." During childhood and adolescence, they begin to discover that there are probably more than two categories of people—six, to be exact. They are: the Skaters, the Preps, the Nerds, the Jocks, the Heads, and the Head-Bangers. You'll need a separate piece of software to define these categories as they are apparently determined by several variables, including musical preference, attire, criminal record, and type of drug abuse. (Jocks, for example, abuse alcohol, while Skaters seem to prefer LSD.)

One afternoon, I happened to overhear one of my daughter's many phone conversations (by the way, she should become a major shareholder of AT&T any day now). She was protesting, "You told him I was a Head-Banger? I'm not! I'm not a Head either! You're a Head!" I felt relieved that she had finally set the record straight.

Later that same day, she corrected me when I asked her about the boyfriend she was "going out" with. Rolling her eyes, she asked me, "Don't you know *anything*?" She explained that she was not "going out" with him; they were "going together." I realized I was in way over my head, a feeling not unlike the way I felt during my college thermodynamics course. (I don't recall the professor being so condescending, though.)

Direct verbal communication with your kids is crucial— and the family contract doesn't eliminate this need. However, because it does clarify your teen's day-to-day expectations and responsibilities, there's time to have conversations on subjects other than dirty dishes and phone privileges. We can then ponder, along with our 15-year-old philosophers, difficult questions such as, "Hey, Dad, like did you ever think that the whole galaxy might just be a part of a neutrino which is part of one of a billion trillion atoms making up a piece of dog food? I mean, like, what would happen if a dog came along and

ate us? Would it, like, cause major earthquakes or what?"
(On second thought, discussing dirty dishes might ultimately be more enlightening.)

But effective communication is not just a problem
between parents and kids. Believe me, communication
between adults isn't much better. Here's an illustration:

When our psychiatric hospital started ROPES, a program designed to solve group communication problems
using a combination of obstacle course workups and
group therapy, the staff was asked to participate in a
day-long training workshop. No problem.

So there we were on this particular Saturday morning
out on the ROPES training course, dressed in our shorts
and tee-shirts, all 12 of us, including M.D.'s, Ph.D.'s,
R.N.'s, and other college-educated types. As soon as the
group settled down, the group leader directed us to form
a circle with one person standing in the center. He asked
us to play a game we've all played as children, where the
person in the middle folds his arms, closes his eyes, and
keeps his feet together while falling backward. He is
then passed from person to person while pivoting on his
heels. We were instructed to pass this person once "this
way" (the leader made an imaginary counter-clockwise
circle with his hands), once "that way" (the leader ges-
tured in the opposite direction), and once "back and forth."

Pretty simple, right? The memorable part was that it
took this group of teachers, business administrators, nurses,
psychiatrists, and psychologists four times to get it right—
we, the experts in communication! (This experience leads
me to believe that the collective IQ of any group of adults is
equal to approximately one-fourth of its average shoe size....)

So there you have it: The "art" of communicating with
your kids—and with each other. But knowing what to
say and how to say it won't necessarily prevent sabotage,
that dastardly clever mechanism that has destroyed
more than one family contract. In fact, there are so
many ways for sabotage to work its poison that I've
devoted a whole chapter to the subject. Read on....

CHAPTER SEVEN

How to Sabotage the Family Contract

At the risk of being accused of oversimplifying, I believe there are three types of people in the world:

- Fixers
- Complainers
- Underminers

Fixers of the world are a rare breed indeed.

Complainers outnumber the fixers about twelve to one—according to the latest Leftin poll.

Underminers are first cousins to the complainers and they will figure out how to sabotage just about anything. Because they are so subtle, these guys can move around the world of the fixers without being noticed—until they've done their dirty work.

Unfortunately, the family contract is not immune to their special brand of sabotage. I know. To prevent this kind of assault on your family contract, I'm going to let you in on the trade secrets of both the underminers and the complainers. If you're one of them and you're out there, the jig is up. The world's about to learn how to sabotage the family contract....

Secret #1: Put the Kids in Charge of It

This one's a sure-fire way to shoot down the family contract even before it gets off the ground. It undermines the very foundation of the contract (which is built on the rather radical concept that Mom and Dad should be running the house). All you have to do is ask the kids what they think of the family contract and let them decide if they want to adopt it for the household. Do be careful, however, not to interrupt their television viewing with this discussion. Wait for a commercial they don't like. Then quickly (you'll only have 30 seconds before Roseanne comes back on) try to explain all about it. Actually 30 seconds will be more than adequate because you'll be interrupted as soon as the kids get the idea that there are going to be rules involved. They may condescend to explain to you why the contract must be rejected out of hand ("it's stupid, dude") or they may simply grunt disapproval. If they don't answer at all, wait for the next commercial and try again. Repeat this process until they're 35 years old.

Secret #2: The Family Tree

Listen to relatives, in-laws, and friends who tell you they never had a family contract when they were kids and look how perfect they turned out. (This one is self-explanatory.)

Secret #3: The Tried and True Clichés

Forget about the contract altogether and rely strictly on sayings from the time-honored Parent's Book of Things to Say to Your Kids. They include such gems as, "I only hope your kids grow up to be as rotten to you as you are to me," and "I'll give you something to cry about."

Secret #4: We Already Tried It

For those of you who prefer a more subtle approach, this technique does the trick with an end run around the idea of the family contract as an ongoing process. "We already tried it" really means, "We tried it for a day and the kids were still spray-painting the refrigerator with Marxist slogans."

This kind of mentality does have its limitations. Those who subscribe to the "we already tried it" school of thought will never, for example, become concert pianists. They give up after the first lesson because no Chopin could be heard whatsoever.

Secret #5: I Told You It Wouldn't Work

A variation of the "we already tried it (for a day)" sabotage is the "we already tried (that one thing)." Let me explain. People who want to undermine the contract using this particular attack will pick one of the rules to try out at home. (The selection process is a scientific one invoking the use of a complex numerology which requires finding the square root of Shirley MacLaine's current age.) When the item of the contract is chosen, let's say "homework," the child is dutifully given five points for doing it. Unfortunately, he has no earthly idea what these points are all about or why he got them and, shrugging, he resumes his spray-painting. The saboteur can now knowingly toss this book into the circular file, finally earning the right to proclaim the Underminer's Pledge of Allegiance: "I told you it wasn't going to work. Just another one of those smart-ass psychiatrists trying to make a quick buck."

Happily, these saboteurs do not come out unscathed. For example, they have bad luck with cars. Every time there is any type of automotive problem, they rotate their tires. (This, of course, does very little for the clogged air filters and broken piston rings.)

Secret #6: Splitting Parents

This is a classic undermining technique, one that is widely used and respected. It is beautiful in its simplicity. Mom tells the kid "black" and Dad tells him "white." One parent emerges as "cool" and the other one is "the bitch."

CLAUSE PAUSE

A Fresh Idea

A friend of mine, a successful hospital adminis-
trator, got around the problem of the ever-popular
complainers' assault by refusing to listen to a com-
plaint from any of his employees unless they also
presented a possible solution at the same time.

Let me elaborate. This is the one where Mom reads
this book and decides to give it a try—but Dad won't go
for it. First of all, reading anything conflicts with his
bowling nights. Dad also happens to feel that if Junior
did give the neighbor's dog LSD, it would probably teach
them to keep Fido chained up in the back yard where he
belongs. Now, Mom, not wanting to upset Dad because
he yells loud enough to peel the wallpaper when he gets
wind of a possible disagreement, strategically hides the
book behind the velvet toreador painting in the living
room. Stoically deciding to "go it alone" in implementing
the contract, she firmly tells Junior that he will not get
his allowance that week because of the Fido incident.
Within minutes, Dad enters the house, all aglow from
having just bowled his first game over 120 (and possibly
also from the six-pack he consumed on the way home.)
He magnanimously decides to share his moment of glory
by spontaneously awarding his son five buckaroos to go
out and "raise some hell." Junior, always the wise investor,
figures he can turn the five into fifty almost overnight if
he uses the money to purchase PCP to feed to all the
neighborhood pets. Hey, it's that positive reinforcement
principle all over again.

Secret #7: I'm Not the One Who Has the Problem

Finally, the most direct way of broadsiding the family
contract right through the guardrail and into the canal

is the so-called "I'm not the one with the problem so I'm not changing a thing I do" technique. Since the contract requires considerable changes in parenting techniques, this one will kill it dead in its tracks. As Machiavelli said, "If you want to see people at their worst, ask them to change."

You now have the tools to set up your own family contract. You can circumvent loopholes, implement revisions, and enforce it with strength. You've learned how the positive techniques of communicating with kids can help your contract—and you've discovered how sabotage can sneak in. There's only one issue left before you can make the family contract your own. It has to do with being a parent—and how that gives you the advantage....

CHAPTER EIGHT

Parenting Issues

In my many group therapy sessions with adolescents (I think of them as fifteen teens against one—me), I've listened to countless variations on the following exchange:

> ME: We're starting a no smoking policy in the program.
> DON: You mean, dude, that just because you say we can't do something that like, we've been doing like for *five* years, like we have to just stop? Just like that, right?
> ME: Right.
> *(Silence, during which five of the adolescents attempt to use telekinetic powers to lift desks off the ground to drop on me. Then, noticing that this is not working, confusion sets in.)*

At the risk of being redundant and repetitive, I present the old-fashioned notion that parents should be in charge of the house, teachers should be in charge of the schools, and therapists should be in charge of their adolescent group therapy sessions.

Let me put it another way: Short of child abuse, when parents and kids cannot agree, parents should win.

Unless a building's foundation is sound, you can forget about how you're going to decorate the 10th floor. Unless parents, as the foundation of the family, are consistent, knowledgeable, and in accord, there's no use even trying to involve the kids in the family contract.

But before we can talk about parenting, we first need
to define who the parental figures are. Sounds simple,
but raising kids is now more complicated than ever—
thanks to 40 percent divorce rates, "blended" families,
and full-time jobs for both parents outside the home. The
traditional concept of biological Mom and Dad as parents is, in today's world, a gross overgeneralization.
About a third of American children now grow up with no
father-figure (not even a step-father) in the home. In
fact, thanks to various legal, financial, and social situations, the functional "parent" might not even be related
to the child. Often *several* parental figures are involved.
As we have seen in Chapter Five, without the participa-
tion of the working parent's day-care provider, the family contract is doomed to fail.

Parenting is all about awareness—and understanding
your role and what place you have in your child's life. In
other words, to understand today's compelling parenting
issues, you first have to understand yourself. To that
end, take a few minutes to do the quiz below. It can go
far in helping your...

"PARENT'S AWARENESS FACTOR"

Think of these statements as food for thought. Look
them over. See if they ring true. Think about your
responses. By focusing in on the questions they raise,
you'll help increase your "Parent's Awareness Factor."

1. I have someone take care of my child during the
   day while I'm at work.
2. I have trouble saying no to my child.
3. When my teen asks me if he can use the car, I
   always tell him to ask his father.
4. I'm a single parent.
5. My ex-husband and I have joint custody of our
   children.
6. Grandparents make the best babysitters.

7. When it comes to discipline, I believe in getting tough.
8. I always try to reason with my child first when she's done something wrong.
9. I hate conflict.
10. I don't remember the last time I got angry.
11. I always make sure I spend a few hours a day with my child.
12. I'm working so hard and so late, I sometimes think my child doesn't even recognize me when I come home.
13. My teen knows exactly how to manipulate me to get what she wants.
14. My word is law around the house.
15. My spouse and I never get a chance to talk in private.

Call them responsibilities. Call them family dynamics. Call them the facts of a parent's life. But whatever you call them, the issues this "Parent's Awareness Factor" quiz raises are the "boilerplates" of the family contract, the generic clauses that must be clarified and understood in order for your family to function happily and well. Let's go over these boilerplates now:

Boilerplate #1: Saying No

Remember the word "no." Nancy Reagan liked it a lot in dealing with teenage drug abuse and Don Regan. It's one of my favorites, too. There are so many applications for such a simple word. Let's practice matching the correct answer with the following questions frequently asked by teenagers:

1. Can I ride my skateboard down the airport parking garage?
2. Can I spend the night with punk singer, Sid Vituperative?
3. Can I rent a limousine with a jacuzzi for the prom?
4. And on and on and on.

Answers:

1. No.
2. No.
3. No.
4. And no and no and no.

I told my daughter she had to learn the meaning of the word "no" and she told me I had to learn the meaning of the word "yes." Funny, yes, but you don't necessarily get points for a sense of humor in a family contract.

It's one thing for my daughter to disagree, but if one parent says "no" and the other says, "I, uh, well, I guess so...as long as you promise not to sell any more crack," the picture gets kind of bleak. You might as well forget about trying to use a family contract unless this particular issue is resolved and both of you are in accord with saying no.

Boilerplate #2: Expressing Anger

I am rather embarrassed to quote the source, but I saw this one on a billboard for liquor. It said, "Success is the best revenge." What that has to do with getting smashed, I really don't know. However, it's an intriguing concept, especially when it comes to your child's emotions.

Think of it: If your teen could deal with his anger by channeling it into his contract, working even harder to "let off steam," he would earn more points and freedom. For example, if he's expounding on how "unfair" it is to have a ten-minute phone limit, you might remind him that if he spent his time and energy complying with the contract rules and chores instead of losing points arguing with you, he could earn Level Four privileges—which include unlimited phone call time. Not only would he be free to chatter on the phone, but he wouldn't have to have these "delightful" discussions about phone privileges in the first place. In short, the family contract will help him learn how to redirect his anger in productive ways, teaching him that consistent hard work is a more effective

CLAUSE PAUSE

Now You See It, Now You Don't

New Jersey high school principal Joe Clark recently won national attention for a get-tough policy at his school. He actually patrols the corridors of learning with a baseball bat. It seems Mr. Clark has the rather radical notion that education is a privilege. He also seems to think that those who come to school to intimidate and disrupt can go back to where they belong: the subway. I don't believe he has ever actually used the bat.

Mr. Clark and his baseball bat reminds me of my father, who simply showed us The Belt from Texas (approximately five feet wide, as I recall) from time to time. He never needed to deploy this intermediate-range armament to restore immediate order in the house. Eventually, we didn't even have to see it. Verbal reminders about its existence (or periodically handing out snapshots of it) seemed sufficient to clarify what had previously seemed to be complicated family issues.

way of achieving privileges than arguing, demanding, manipulation, and testing limits.

But sometimes it isn't enough to mow the lawn with a vengeance and add up those privilege points. Sometimes your child is so angry that he needs to vent it in a direct, physical way. If the thought of exercise falls on deaf ears (despite its point-ability), tell your child it's okay to hit something soft like a mattress—provided no one is hurt and nothing is damaged. Even screaming and yelling can be okay at the right time and place. If you look closely, you will notice that many rush hour commuters stuck in traffic are already using this technique. (And you thought they were all just singing along with the radio.)

Shadow punching. Door slamming. Yelling. Running. Threats and ultimatums. Arguments and heated discussions. Racing through the day on overload. All these signs of anger are easy to detect; all can be channeled in more positive ways. But there is one kind of anger that is much more subtle—and unhealthy.

It's called passive-aggression, which is jargon for an immature way of expressing anger. Procrastination, "forgetting," sloppiness, and laziness are all examples of passive-aggressive behavior. In Chapter Two, I recounted the story of a little boy who refused to go to school and got away with it. His maternal grandmother drove him to the schoolyard every day, only to turn around and take him home when he started making a fuss.

I used this story to illuminate how kids get away with much too much these days. But there's more to this tale. It's also a quintessential study in passive-aggression. Here's why:

The boy's mother was divorced, and as with many other single working parents, she relied heavily on Grandma to help raise her son. Unfortunately, neither she nor Grandma recognized the anger that this situation provoked. Nor could they see that it was this angry climate that caused the boy to "act out" and refuse to go to school. As she subsequently discovered during the therapy process, Grandma felt horribly put upon. She resented having to raise a child at her age; she felt she had already paid her dues in the child-rearing department. But rather than deal directly with this anger and discuss it with her daughter, she suppressed it.

But suppressing anger doesn't make it go away. Instead, she became passive-aggressive—by driving her grandson home as soon as he said he didn't want to go to school. Just to make sure the angry message was perfectly clear without having to say a word, Grandma bought the boy ice cream, which he ate while watching television cartoons.

Needless to say, when Mom saw them, she became infuriated. There were Grandma and her son finishing off the last of the Blue Bell Vanilla in front of the TV. In a rather well orchestrated way, the little boy and his grandmother simultaneously shrugged their shoulders to apologize.

When Mom finally got angry enough to do something about the problem, they all began family therapy with me. Note that I treated the *family*—not just the little boy. If I had repeatedly asked him why he didn't want to go to school, he probably would have given me that same well-rehearsed shoulder shrug. From his point of view, school refusal made very good sense. Why go to school where you have to sit through two hours of arithmetic when you can watch Road Runner and eat ice cream at home?

The kid had a point. However, once his mom and his grandma were able to confront their problems, they were able to work out a routine whereby Grandma had fewer parenting responsibilities. Mom took over more of the role that should have been hers all along. The moral of the story? The boy got better—and goes off to school every day without a hitch.

Boilerplate #3: Minimizing the Splitting Syndrome

If one parent continues to say yes while the other says no, splitting will occur. You remember, that's when one parent is "cool" and the other is a "jerk." (See Chapter Seven.)

Officially, splitting is a child's technique to get parents to fight with each other—and, believe it or not, it happens to be normal. Unfortunately, it's usually very effective. Here's an example:

Timmy asks Dad for money to go to the movies. Dad says no. Timmy then asks Mom, who gives him the money. Dad is angry and resentful; he feels his authority has been undermined; he doesn't like being in the role of the bad guy. One or two things may happen:

1. Mom and Dad have a big fight, or...
2. ...Dad takes a passive-aggressive stance and relinquishes responsibility—not only for this situation, but for *all* situations. "If you're not going to

let me have any authority with the kids, I'm also not going to take any of the responsibility for what they do."

(Why Mom said yes to begin with presents a whole set of other problems. She might have been unaware that her husband had already said no. Or she might be fully aware of the situation, but because she's angry at him for something else, she's decided to play the passive-aggressive game and say, yes.)

But why does splitting occur? Why do children engage in trying to split their parents in the first place? Is it because their purpose on earth is to drive parents straight up the nearest available wall? Are they really that sadistic?

Hopefully not. There is another possible explanation. It could be a kid's way of finding out if Mom and Dad talk to each other, if they are happily in sync. Good communication translates directly into security. But every disagreement or fight a child overhears is fraught with the fear that his parents are going to split up and abandon him. This anxiety is a fact of life in young children and causes them to keep their parents under constant surveillance—by periodically checking out the climate via this "splitting syndrome." It's as if the child is floating in a lifeboat (his parents) and feels compelled every so often to poke at its hull just to make sure it's not going to spring a leak. I don't believe children do this consciously. (Then again, probably the only fully conscious things kids do is play the very popular Nintendo video game, Mario Brothers II.) But whether or not a child knows what he's doing here is almost beside the point. What is important is the fact that his fear and anxiety will only intensify if there is any sign of trouble, if the boat "springs a leak."

Unfortunately, in today's world, these signs of trouble are very common. In fact, splitting takes on a whole new meaning when it is used between divorced parents. Listen to this grim scenario:

After the divorce, Billy lived with Mom until he became

CLAUSE PAUSE

Other Splits

Splitting isn't always a parental phenomenon. A child can use it between any two authority figures. When, for instance, Johnny comes home with an F in biology and complains to Mom that it's because of Mr. Quigmire's poor teaching skills, she immediately calls the principal, demanding Quigmire's resignation. Johnny has successfully split Mom against teacher. (He has also conveniently forgotten to tell her that the last time he did any homework whatsoever was during the Pre-Cambrian Era.)

---

unmanageable. When he had a keg party in the backyard, Mom put her foot down and insisted that in the future he would have to limit the number of kegs per person to no more than two. Billy then delivered the ultimate threat: "Well, I'll just go live with Dad."

This new living arrangement lasted about a month, during which time Mom remarried. Meanwhile, back at Dad's house, Billy set fire to Dad's favorite reclining chair. Despite Billy's protests that at least nobody was sitting in it at the time, Dad has had enough—and Billy is shipped back to Mom's for a surprise homecoming.

This Ping-Pong style of parenting continues for, say, two or three years, during which time Billy's behavior goes from bad to worse. When everyone gets tired of playing this back-and-forth game, the family genius in residence, usually a brother-in-law, figures out the solution to the whole mess: military school. This option works for some kids. Others get booted out of military school for the same reasons they were sent. They emerge with the same behavioral problems, except now the know how to launch a surface-to-air missile.

The good news is that there is a cure for splitting.

Simply make it a contract rule that if you say no, your child is not allowed to ask your spouse the same question—unless he informs the other parent that you have already said no.

To avoid splitting altogether, good communication skills between parents are crucial. It all comes down to the fine art of...

Boilerplate #4: Negotiating

There are always at least two sides to every issue. Kurosawa's famous film *Rashomon,* opens with a murder witnessed by several people. Throughout the movie, these witnesses describe what they saw and heard; each one, of course, has a significantly different account. This movie eloquently makes the point that we see events from our own unique perspective. In my not so eloquent way, I would say this is because we are people, not video cameras.

It is these different perspectives that make negotiating between parents so important. Many spouses find that while they agree on everything in principle, they can't agree on anything when it gets down to the nitty-gritty.

As Lily Tomlin says in her play, *Search for Signs of Intelligent Life in the Universe,* "I always knew I was going to be somebody, but now I realize I should have been more specific." Most parents agree children should be raised with love and discipline, but the family contract provides a way to "be more specific." Parents will agree that Sam should take care of his dog, but they can't seem to get it together enough to agree that this means bringing Cookie to the vet. They'll agree that Belinda should be home at a "reasonable hour" on school nights, but they can't determine what that hour should be. They'll agree that Sam should clean his room, but not whether that includes vacuuming the bedroom rug once a week. They'll agree that Belinda should only associate with "positive" friends, but they don't know whether this includes her buddy Joanne or not. In fact, they can't even agree on how specific their family contract should be....

Negotiating isn't easy, but it isn't impossible either. There are some steps you can take to make it work:

1. Set aside time for the negotiation process. If you are a single parent and not suffering from a dreaded multiple personality disorder, negotiations should be relatively speedy. For those of you who must negotiate with a spouse, be sure you are talking to your spouse alone—and in total privacy. In most households this will mean literally behind closed doors. (Sometimes even closing the doors isn't good enough. Alyson and I recently learned that conversations we held in our bedroom were, thanks to the air conditioning duct, audible in the kids' bathroom. We discovered this "leak" at the same time we noticed that our daughter, age 7, always seemed to describe her feelings about the latest boost in our property taxes with exactly the same adjectives I had chosen the night before.)

2. Allow adequate time for your meeting. For example, parents who try to fit negotiating in on the drive to the supermarket will not only botch the family contract, but will end up so confused that they often accidentally purchase gefilte fish. Don't assume the entire contract must be completed in one meeting. It's okay to disagree. Even Reagan and Gorbachev didn't hit it off in Reykjavik at their first summit meeting—and they didn't even have to share a bathroom.

3. As the first disagreements start to fly, stop and listen before you speak. Psychobabblists talk a lot about "active listening" these days. For me, this conjures up a visual image of one of those toy dogs in the car's rear windshield with its head oscillating at about 120 cycles per minute. When people listen like this, they too bounce their heads, usually while saying such pearls as, "Yes, I know exactly how you feel." They rock from foot to foot waiting for the first opportunity to jump in and "share...."

Instead, I would recommend "passive listening," which means three things:

1. Don't talk for at least five seconds after your spouse completes a sentence. (It's a lot tougher than most people realize.)

2. Establish and maintain eye contact
3. Imagine yourself in your spouse's shoes (unless they're wearing those furry slippers with Bugs Bunnytoes)

When these three rules are closely followed, many people find that their spouse who "never talks" actually has quite a lot to say.

4. Try to find at least one point in your spouse's position that sounds reasonable—and start your response with it. When people feel they've been heard and taken seriously, they tend to listen better themselves— and they're more prone to compromise. In my work, I listen to patients pour out their thoughts and feelings all the time. By the end of the session, they sometimes thank me for helping them—although I gave them no profound insights or advice. They felt better simply because they felt they had been heard and understood. In that frame of mind, they'll usually find solutions to their problems themselves.

To give you an idea of the fine art of negotiating in action, here are two imaginary scenarios in which Mom and Dad attempt to reach a compromise on Johnny's evening curfew:

SCENARIO ONE

SETTING: Mom and Dad are watching *Geraldo* in the living room.

MOM: That kid needs to be in by a reasonable hour every night. I'm sick and tired of his coming home at all hours smelling like smoke. And I just bought him a new shirt, $35 for a Calvin Klein shirt, and do you think he cares? It stinks already from cigarettes. Let him wash it.

DAD: I, uh...

Geraldo: Welcome to the show. Tonight we'll be talking to some of the famous Los Angeles freeway shooters to ask the question, "What makes these slimeballs tick, anyway?"

MOM: You don't see Tommy Stevens coming in with a smelly shirt. He's got a racquetball scholarship to Yale. You don't see him come waltzing home at 2 AM. You know why, Harold? Because he's got a father who doesn't take any bull. *His* father knows how to crack the whip and boy, does that kid jump. You *never* crack the whip, do you Harold? You expect me to do all the work around here *and* keep the kids in line. It would be nice if, just once, you helped me out around here and started cracking the whip.

DAD: I, uh...

Geraldo (to his guest on the show): ... and you think that just because the woman's bumper sticker said "Visualize World Peace," that gives you the right to pull out your Uzi and start firing, huh?

Phone rings. Mom answers, talks to her best friend, Shirley, for 45 minutes.

MOM (to Shirley): Yeah, Jean doesn't seem to know when to just get up from the barstool and walk out when Bill starts making a scene. Well, I've got to get going now. Harold and I are in the middle of a real important talk about Johnny. I'm trying to get Harold to wake up and realize that if he keeps wimping out on me his son is going to end up in serious trouble. See you later. Call me in ten minutes and I'll let you know if Harold has seen the light yet.

Geraldo (Commercial): Feel the rich Corinthian leather.

MOM: I'm surprised you stayed awake for a change. What did I miss on *Geraldo*? You know we really have to get this thing with Johnny straightened out. I'm sick of telling him over and over and over not to smoke and to come in at a decent hour. Why don't you do it for a change? Sure, you just want to let me do all the dirty work for you.

DAD: I, uh...

MOM: Well, I'm sick of it. Do you know how much that

shirt of his cost? Take a guess. You don't know do
you because you never take him shopping, do you?
That's a Calvin Klein shirt and it cost $35. How is
he supposed to care if his father doesn't care either?

Geraldo: tune in next week when we will broadcast
live and on-site to explore the undiscovered treasures
of the U-Haul Storage Rental space of none other
than the late Jimmy Hoffa.

DAD: I care.

MOM: Oh, sure you care. All you care about is that
damn boat of yours. When I think about all the
money we've sunk into that thing, I...

DAD: Oh yeah? Well what about that bill from Niemann's
yesterday? What's the matter, you in competition
with Imelda Marcos for the "Most Shoes Award," or
what?

SCENARIO TWO

SETTING: Mom and Dad are sitting in the living room
alone, facing one another. No radio, no TV. Silence.

MOM: That kid needs to be in by a reasonable hour
every night. I'm sick and tired of his coming home
at all hours. What do you think about a 9:00 curfew?
(Pause 5 seconds while Dad is thinking.)

DAD: I was thinking more like 11.

Phone rings, Mom answers, talks to her best friend,
Shirley for 20 seconds.

MOM: Shirley, I'll call you back in about half an hour.
Harold and I are in the middle of something right
now, O.K.? Talk to you later.

MOM: Why do you think 11?

DAD: I think most kids his age get home around that
time.

MOM: Look, I understand. You're saying it's important
for him to have friends and we don't want to interfere
with his social life too much, right?

DAD: Basically, yes. And I think he can probably handle
11 just fine.

MOM: Yes, he's basically a mature kid. But I really think 11 is just a bit late. Can we compromise? How about 10?

DAD: I guess so.

MOM: We can put 10:00 curfew in the contract then, right?

DAD: Right.

MOM: Will you tell him about this, then, starting tomorrow?

DAD: Sure. You want to watch *Geraldo?*

Obviously, Scenario Two is the most desirable. Unfortunately, many parents get stuck in Scenario One. Therefore, the first person to enforce curfews in Johnny's life will be his drill sergeant or his probation officer. But, unless Scenario Two-type negotiating can take place, the information in this book will have an approximate value of one peso. If you and your spouse are stuck in a Scenario One situation, I strongly recommend marital therapy before attempting to start the family contract with the kids.

Boilerplate #5: Setting Priorities

No parent would disagree that it's important to spend time with the kids. But action speaks louder than words. Many of these same parents find all kinds of reasons why they "can't."

In fact, many of these parents would also complain that they don't have time to even think about finding time to be with their kid.

How is this situation justified? With "quality time" —which I'm beginning to feel is another psychobabble-type rationalization for not spending enough time with our kids. A parent who schedules his kids in for an hour a week to have a "quality time talking feelings" with them is deluding himself; he is simply acting out his guilt for his unavailability.

Whatever happened to "quantity time"? Ironically, spending those extra hours with one's family is, in the

CLAUSE PAUSE

I'm Okay, You're Not So Hot

Here's a lesson I learned from a senior psychiatrist during my training. An irate patient had just broken his nose. Always seeking to understand human emotion, I asked the psychiatrist "how he felt" about the incident. He thought for a while and uttered this profound reply: "I wanted to kill the sonofabitch." I have come to treasure this memory as one of the highlights of my psychiatric training. I learned that it's okay even for psychiatrists to get mad.

long run, more time efficient. (Picking up your kid at the police station and driving him to his appointments with his probation officer because his license was revoked can be rather time-consuming.)

Successful parents understand that daily interaction with their kids, from playing a game of checkers to reading a goodnight story, is infinitely more valuable than trying to get reacquainted in a once a week "quality time" encounter crammed in between tennis, dinner with the boss, and entertaining clients from out of town.

In therapy, I try to help modern parents get their priorities in order. I try to reframe the "can't's" into the "choices" they really are—choices a parent makes between work and family time.

In a recent telephone survey of 1200 parents conducted by the Massachusetts Mutual Life Insurance Corporation, 63 percent listed their families as their greatest source of pleasure. When asked what was the single greatest reason for the decline of family life, 35 percent said parents don't spend enough time with their families. Yet when the same group was asked if they would take a job that would raise their family income by 15 percent, but would take them away from their family even more, about two-thirds said they would take the job.

Over the years, an interesting phenomenon has come to light. Approximately 1500 patients have attempted to convince me of the same thing: their job is unique. They are the only ones that can run things at the office the way they should be run. They are the only ones whose clients and customers would forget all about them if they didn't go out with them at a moment's notice.

An interesting quandary indeed—and one with a deceptively simple solution. It all comes down to either choosing a big house, a big-screen TV, and big problems with the kids—or choosing a small house, a small TV, and small problems with the kids.

I am able to convince some parents that life goes on without jacuzzis and new cars. Some even begin to see that they must look inward to understand the source of "I can't"—instead of blaming external pressures. They begin to explore the real reasons for their workaholic tendencies, including a fear of intimacy with their own family, a preoccupation with material possessions, and an unconscious wish to please their own parents....

Working out a family contract takes time and commitment. You need to set priorities before you start and make the choices that are right for you and your family.

Boilerplate #6: Role Modeling

Time is more than quality versus quantity. Parents need time not only for their kids, but for their spouses, their own parents and siblings, their friends, their creative pursuits, their exercise and relaxation programs, and, yes, even fun.

Not only will this give *you* a healthier and happier life (not to mention more time to spend with the family), but you'll also be providing your child with a positive role model. A dependent child naturally looks up to her parents. For healthy, normal development, a child needs parents to be positive role models, people whose lives appear balanced and reasonable. It's difficult, for example, to lecture your teen about the need for exercise when you're 30 pounds overweight. It's almost impossible to tell your teen not to smoke when you're flicking your cigarette ash as you speak.

(I recall that when I was seduced by the workaholicism myth, I was seeing more patients per week in my practice than Carl Jung saw in his entire lifetime. I would advise my patients to keep their priorities straight, to exercise regularly, to be sure to get enough sleep, and so on. Observant patients didn't take the advice seriously and kept saying that I looked tired. Recently the Institute for The Living, a noted psychiatric facility in Hartford, Connecticut, has begun a specific program for workaholic professionals. I'm checking in for a while as soon as I finish this chapter.)

Boilerplate #7: Enforcing What You Believe

Back in college, I was once playing chess with a guy who, as they say in chess lingo, was "whipping my ass." Suddenly I saw a move that looked like a winner, and without hesitation, I made it. I then sat back smugly, waiting for my now pathetic opponent to lose. But as I glanced down at the board, I realized that the move I had just made was really a terrible one. I had inadvertently put my queen right in front of his pawn. (My chess rating has been compared to that of the upper range for invertebrates.)

It was obvious that all my opponent had to do was take my queen with his pawn—and win the game. But he didn't see the pawn *either*. In retrospect, I saw that it was the *way* I had made my move that counted. In my false belief that I had actually won the game, I conveyed decisiveness and certainty in my body language. I won because I had *believed* in my move.

True belief is just as important when it comes to parenting. For one thing, kids are able to perceive the parental bluff in about .04 nanoseconds. Secondly, if you don't believe what you are saying or in what you are trying to enforce, I guarantee that you'll eventually back down—either from your kids' badgering and campaigning or from their guilt trips or full-blown Toltec Indian war dance temper tantrums. Unfortunately, recanting your decision under these circumstances sends a clear message to your child that pressure tactics—and *not* compliance with the contract rules—can get him anything he wants (including all the major credit cards).

As with my game of chess, your gestures, your body language, and your tone of voice must all convey confidence and decisiveness.

This attitude doesn't mean that you believe that you are always right and have all the answers. But it does mean that you can trust your own judgment enough, that your maturity and experience count for something, and that, if you have the responsibility of raising your kids, you also have the right to have the final say. You might make mistakes, but you believe they'll be much more benign and reversible than the mistakes your kids would make if they were allowed to raise themselves solo.

Remember this parent's credo. It will help you feel confident and in control—without false bravado and without an unhealthy sense of infallibility.

Boilerplate #8: Disciplining When All Else Fails

You've remained calm and consistent. You've explained the consequences of your child's actions. You've taken away his privileges—and you've kept to the Level One restrictions. But your child is still not listening. He's not complying with the family contract....

There's still one other option. A last-resort method of enforcing your family contract is the use of physical force. But it should be used only if you are physically capable of restraining your child—and there is no risk of injury to anyone. (Therefore, a slap in a rebellious adolescent's face is not the kind of physical force I'm talking about. It also happens to be illegal.)

Spanking can work for young children under 7 years of age. (Trying to spank a kid older than that results in something that faintly resembles a medieval fraternity hazing. It also leaves both parent and child humiliated and feeling even further apart from each other.)

Personally, I must confess, I do not favor spanking. Sometimes I think it's more effective as an outlet for a parent's anger than as a disciplinary tool. It also fosters the belief that violence is okay—and an acceptable way to handle disputes.

What then is the alternative? It's called "the holding technique" and, as Jay Haley describes in his book *Techniques of Family Therapy,* it's an effective way to deal with your child's temper tantrums. Here's how it works:

Let's say that your child's TV time is up for the day. You inform him of this fact and he ignores you (which helps him lose points in the "Attitude and Behavior" rule.) Being careful not to repeat yourself, you get up from your chair and turn off the television. Your child turns it back on. You then tell him to go to his room. He refuses. You take him by the hand and begin walking him to his room. He pulls his hand away, walks to his room without your help, and slams the door closed. He begins throwing his toys around the room, careening his F-14 model jet off the wall and ceiling for a dramatic, yet realistic, test flight. After a few minutes of this, he walks out of his room, struts over to the television—and turns it back on to *The Partridge Family.* (You know, the one where Sissy gets to keep the cocker spaniel after all.)

Rather than pull out your hair (or the hair of your child), simply go to the kitchen. Make yourself some sandwiches and some nonalcoholic drinks. Make a bathroom pit stop. Turn on the telephone answering machine or disconnect the phone. Grab a portable TV or radio, gather up some newspapers, and bring everything into your child's room. (Earplugs will also come in handy.) Lay the newspapers on the floor. Set the drinks and sandwiches nearby. Turn on the TV or radio to something you like, but something that you know your kid will absolutely hate, like *The MacNeil-Lehrer Report.*

CLAUSE PAUSE

The Dread Word: Boredom!

Take away a child's television privileges and she will immediately complain that without TV she's "bored." Oh no, *not that!* Calmly remind your child that you are not her home entertainment center. Pull out a copy of the family contract and, for the twentieth time, read her the list of chores and activities she can do to earn points—which will not only help her regain TV privileges, but relieve her boredom as well.

Now go back into the living room. Pick up your child and carry him (most likely kicking and screaming) into the bedroom. Sit down *on the floor* behind him so that when he screams the sound waves will not directly enter your ear canal. This prevents rupture of the tympanic membrane and possible fractures of the hammer, anvil, and stirrup. (This is also where the earplugs come in handy.) Be sure you have positioned yourself behind your child so that when he kicks, he is only kicking the air—not your shins. Hold his arms firmly (and low enough on the abdomen so your arms and hands are well beyond biting range.) Use only enough physical force to prevent your child from getting away—no more and no less.

After about half an hour of screaming, yelling, kicking, and cursing (you have now finished the tuna and have learned to lip read from Jim Lehrer), your child will begin to cry profusely. You will feel like a sadistic evil being for victimizing such an innocent little creature, but don't let go just yet. Let him cry for a few more minutes—until he stops long enough to listen. Using your calmest tone, reassure your child that you will release him as soon as possible, but not before *you* feel

he is ready. Tell him calmly that the specific criteria for
his release are one, he listens to you, two, the TV is
restricted until further notice, and three, he must stay
in his room for an hour without being destructive. You
will most likely have to repeat this message several
times because your child will begin squirming, crying,
and pleading anew. When you feel he might be ready to
comply with your criteria, let him go. If he goes right
back into the living room and turns the TV on, repeat
the entire process. Eventually, after a few hours, your
child will be ready to obey.

Fun way to spend an evening, right? But the beauty of
this technique is that it usually has to be done only
once. If your child is convinced that you are fully prepared
to use the "holding technique," he'll never push you that
far again.

Some people would consider this technique sadistic or
cruel. I don't agree. A parent's inability to stop a temper
tantrum in motion can result in physical injury—but not
so this technique. (One of my patients, a 14-year-old
girl, expressed a lot of regret about having thrown a can
of tuna at her mom in the middle of an argument. She
missed her mother's head by a few inches. This is why,
at our house, everything is Tupperware and Saran Wrap.)
Besides, being held can also be quite comforting—especially
when you're upset.

Like most things in life, however, the holding technique
is not a cure-all. Some children might be too big or
tall—and their parents won't be able physically to restrain
them. And, in some other cases, it simply won't work. The
kids will continue to have temper tantrums, and the
holding technique is no longer a powerful "last resort"
method of disciplining. When all else fails, the next step is
professional help.

You now have everything you need to create and enforce
a family contract in your home. But before I write "The
End" and leave you to it, there are two more arenas that
must be explored, two "special clauses" that need to be
addressed—especially in today's turbulent times.

CHAPTER 9

Teen Trouble: Drug and Alcohol Abuse

Tina, one of my adult patients, told me a story:

When she was 14, her parents allowed her to smoke marijuana and drink alcohol in their home. They also allowed her friends to do the same. It was only when Tina began shooting up heroin did her parents feel it was time to intervene. (I might add that Tina was not from an inner-city ghetto, but from an extremely wealthy suburban town.) In Tina's family, walking through the living room smoking a joint didn't raise an eyebrow, but pulling out a syringe and shooting up in the kitchen seemed to do the trick. (Actually, it's a little unclear what the "last straw" was—the act of shooting up itself or the destruction of Mom's microwave when Tina used it to try to sterilize her needles.)

To quote from Arthur Miller's play *Death of a Salesman*, "Attention must be paid": to Tina, to other adolescents in similar circumstances, and to a problem that continues to escalate among our young.

THE EXPENSIVE GOODS

There's no illness more misunderstood than alcoholism and drug abuse. The very terminology stirs controversy. What defines an "alcoholic" or a "substance abuser" anyway? Even the experts can't agree. But this confusion over semantics is simply a reflection of the deeper and more somber fact that society still regards these disorders with fear and prejudice.

The weapon against this situation is knowledge—and the understanding it brings. To that end, let's briefly discuss the prevalent drugs in use among teens today—and why.

ALCOHOL, THE DRUG OF CHOICE

Why do some people have such a hard time recognizing alcohol as one of the most addictive and medically dangerous drugs in existence? Probably because it is abused so widely. As the saying goes, they don't know who discovered water, but they're pretty sure it wasn't a fish. Through accidents and medical complications, alcohol kills about 150,000 Americans each year.

In fact, nine out of every ten high school seniors have had at least one drink. For those of you who still doubt that alcohol is a drug, I would point out that alcohol withdrawal carries a much greater mortality rate than heroin withdrawal, that half of the auto fatalities in this country were alcohol-related, and that due to its potent physically addicting properties, more and more young people are getting drunk on the average of every other week.

Alcoholism remains one of psychiatry's greatest challenges. No longer regarding it as a simple moral issue where one's abstinence implies strength, modern psychiatry deals with the much bigger and complicated picture. Brought into focus to formulate effective treatment are:

1. Hereditary patterns. While we have long known that alcoholism runs in families, it is only recently that we've been able to prove that this is due, at least partially, to genetic factors. At least four major studies have found that if one identical twin is an alcoholic, the other has a much greater chance of becoming an alcoholic himself than if the twins were merely fraternal. Even more telling is Dr. Donald Goodwin's discovery that children of alcoholics who are raised as foster children by nonalcoholic parents are still four times more likely to become alcoholics than the natural children of nonalcoholic parents.

2. Biochemical causes include genetic underactivity of alcohol dehydrogenase, a liver enzyme which breaks down alcohol. Oriental people and women have a deficiency in this enzyme—and, consequently, a lower tolerance for alcohol. Antabuse is a medication that blocks this alcohol dehydrogenase; it causes severe nausea, vomiting, heart palpitations, sweating, and flushing if combined with alcohol. Many alcoholics use Antabuse as "insurance" to combat the impulse to drink.

3. Medical complications. Unfortunately, alcohol has serious and direct toxicity to virtually every organ in the human body. It can cause anemia, numbness in the extremities, hepatitis, cirrhosis, bleeding gastric ulcers, heart failure and, within the brain, loss of memory, visual-spatial skills, intellectual function, coordination, and balance. Alcoholism can also cause mood changes and overall personality alteration.

4. Psychological issues. As we have seen in Chapter Two, a child's family history does not absolutely predetermine whether he is destined to become depressed, suicidal, or alcoholic. He might be predisposed to an illness, but only psychological and environmental stresses can trigger it. I have seen many people with strong alcoholic family histories who never develop the problem themselves. On the other hand, there are millions of alcoholics with absolutely no family history of alcoholism at all.

What makes alcoholism so insidious for parents is that it usually begins in the teenage years. Young men with a genetic disposition tend to have a higher tolerance for alcohol; they can "drink their buddies under the table" without getting sick themselves. They also experience more of a "high" than their other friends.

Unfortunately, too, an alcoholic will treat his problem

with more alcohol. Symptoms of withdrawal are practically indistinguishable from anxiety. They include heart palpitations, sweating, muscle tensions, shaking, dizziness, and difficulty sleeping. An alcoholic will attribute these symptoms to "nerves" and, quite correctly, note that when he drinks, the shaking stops. He can relax and finally get some sleep. He doesn't feel drunk, just normal again.

A KICK FROM COCAINE

Cocaine abuse—while declining in overall numbers—still remains a problem for teenagers and young adults. And with cocaine comes tragedy. We have already seen a marked upsurge in fatal heart attacks in people under thirty, including athletes in peak physical condition, such as Len Bias and Don Rogers.

What makes cocaine so deadly lies in its power. It becomes a potent addiction. Laboratory experiments have shown that the cravings for cocaine will supersede the survival instinct. Laboratory rats consistently chose to press a bar to deliver cocaine over food and water—to the point where they died of malnutrition and dehydration. The human corollary is when an intelligent human being forsakes all common sense to walk into a house full of armed drug dealers in a battle zone neighborhood, plunks down the last $400 in his bank account for an unknown substance he is told is cocaine, and begins snorting, smoking, or shooting it up—all the while knowing it might kill him on the spot. The grip of cocaine addiction is so strong that, in a desperate attempt to treat it, some Central American countries have even tried psychosurgery on cocaine addicts, but without success.

The reason cocaine is so addictive relates to its ability to release massive amounts of chemical messengers (called neurotransmitters) in the brain, especially one called dopamine—which immediately goes to work on the "pleasure centers" of the brain. The release of all that dopamine gives the brain a "let's party" message in

CLAUSE PAUSE

Defining Abuse

Here are the general characteristics that mental health professionals use to determine if someone is abusing alcohol or drugs:

- The pattern of use, including morning "fixes," secret drinking, and frequent drug-taking.
- The amount consumed.
- The effect of drinking or drug-taking on a person's intellect, mood, and personality.
    —Job or school performance.
    —Social relationships with friends and family.
- The legal consequences, if any.
- The medical complications—which are almost always present in an abuser.

bright neon. It consequently causes intense euphoria and a sense of well-being, or, to put it even more simply, the high.

But Mother Nature has a way of making sure we don't get something for nothing. (In fact, sometimes I think anything that tastes good or feels good is probably bad for you. I remember reading once that taking hot showers can cause skin cancer. Apparently the heat of the water turns the chlorine into some sort of carcinogen. Great. Something else to worry about besides radon gas in our homes.) Here's the rub: When cocaine is used chronically, the dopamine stores in the brain become depleted. Low levels of dopamine lead to an intense craving for more cocaine; it also causes severe depression. In fact, suicide attempts are not infrequent during a "crash" phase.

FINDING ECSTASY AND MORE IN THE DRUGSTORE

A particularly frightening new development on the drug scene is the so-called "designer" drugs, synthesized to be thousands of times more potent than anything found in nature. Ecstasy or "X" is one such drug. A batch of this particular poison was recently responsible for the development of acute Parkinson's disease in several people in their twenties in California—a disease that's extremely rare in young adults.

One of the main risks of Ecstasy and other designer drugs is that they truly are unknown substances. They are cooked up in apartment kitchens which are converted into makeshift laboratories by chemists from your local Hells Angel chapter. Because these people are, shall we say, motivated to get out of the kitchen heat as soon as possible, they often take shortcuts in the college chemistry cookbooks, creating totally new and unidentified isomers. (If you don't know what an isomer is, don't feel bad. Neither does the dealer on the street. All he knows is that it's "good stuff" and it sells for $20 a hit.)

For reasons that defy all Darwinian logic about our will to survive, kids believe the dealer and buy the stuff. They will refuse to eat the dinner Mom cooked, but they will pay for and consume poison capsules provided by a total strange whose appearance is reminiscent of the foreground character in Edvard Munch's famous lithograph, "The Scream." (One picture is worth a thousand words. If you take the time to find this picture, visualize this character in leather.)

Marijuana is more generic than designer. It's been around a long, long time. Although its use (along with LSD and amphetamines) appears to have leveled off over the past ten years, it's still frequently abused. Don't let its so-called "harmless" reputation fool you. Due to hybrid breeding, marijuana now has about 10 times the THC (active ingredient) concentration of marijuana sold 10 years ago. Marijuana can cause addiction, bronchitis, memory loss, decreased immunity to viral infections, lung cancer, and "amotivational syndrome" (when a person is content to stare at reruns of *The Donna Reed Show* all day).

"Downers" have also been around the block. They include drugs such as Mandrax, Quaaludes, barbiturates, and meprobamate. "Downers" simulate the symptoms of alcohol intoxication and withdrawal; a teen under their influence will invite the risk of seizures, respiratory arrest, and suffocation due to the propensity to vomit while asleep.

RESISTING ARREST

"I don't have a problem."

"It's funny. I don't remember anything after we got in the car to go home. Guess I had a couple too many drinks, but, hey, so did everybody else."

"I can stop whenever I want."

These teens all have two things in common. They have a problem with abusing alcohol or drugs. They also have a problem with the problem. Through denial, excuses, and rationalization, they are resisting treatment. To make matters worse, these same obstacles for help also make substance abuse hard to detect—even in the most responsible of families. Let's go over them now:

●Denying the Undeniable

We all use denial at one time or another in our lives. One of the major tenets of Alcoholics Anonymous is to confront, almost immediately, the natural tendency to deny the existence of an illness. Members often introduce themselves as, "My name is John and I am an alcoholic."

The most striking example of denial I ever witnessed occurred when I was in medical school. I had been doing a rotation on the cancer ward when one of our patients was diagnosed with lung cancer. We sat with the patient for about an hour, during which time the resident discussed, in great detail, the patient's cancer and the treatment plan; he even showed him his chest X rays (which clearly depicted his tumor.) During rounds the next day, we again met with the patient, this time to begin the first phase of treatment. The patient, however, had no idea what we were talking about. He had absolutely no recollection of talking to us at all just the day before.

This patient had no neurological memory problem. He was of average intelligence. And I'm convinced he wasn't lying. He had totally "forgotten" our entire conversation via denial.

Sometimes in the middle of combat a soldier will not even realize he is wounded. Only when the battle subsides and the danger lessens does he feel the pain. It's as if nature has designed us to survive at all costs. If the soldier was distracted by pain, he might not have been able to aim his rifle accurately enough to defend himself. By the same token, a teenager abusing alcohol or drugs is wounded by addiction—and he can't deal with the very real pain and fear that withdrawal conjures up. With the unconscious act of denial, we can deal with emotional pain, especially the anxiety and fear of death, by essentially not dealing with it.

But kids on drugs are not the only ones who have made denial a fine art. Parents, too, are guilty. Let's face it. There is nothing that will produce more anxiety in a parent than a threat to his or her child. The thought of losing a child, to most parents, is even more frightening than contemplating their own death. In fact, the thought is so frightening that denial is unconsciously and automatically employed. To think about our children getting AIDS, for example, stirs up so much fear it is truly overwhelming and must be repressed. Denial takes away the fear. Unfortunately, in keeping us from thinking about the problem, it also keeps us from taking steps to prevent disaster.

Take one mother, for instance, who told me that, although she had never actually discovered her son smoking marijuana, she did notice that he had put a lock on his door. He kept a fan and a can of air freshener in his room; he also seemed to buy a lot of Visine and breath mints. In medical school, we had a saying that if

---

CLAUSE PAUSE

Searching the Room

If you suspect your child is taking drugs, it's tempting to search his room—but it's also a difficult decision to make. While there is no question that such an invasion of privacy can damage trust between parent and child, remember that your child's credibility has already been damaged enough to get you to this point.

If you do decide to check it out, be prepared for some unpleasant surprises. And, above all, don't do it in secret. Announce the search immediately prior to doing it. (As a last-ditch effort to leave him with some credibility, you may want to give your child a chance to show you any drugs, alcohol, or automatic weapons he may have hidden in the room before you actually begin the search.)

---

we see an animal with four legs and a tail that looks like a horse, it's probably a horse. It could be a zebra. Maybe the kid just values his privacy, likes fresh air, needs Visine for allergies, and has bad breath. Maybe. But it's probably a horse.

●Secrets and Secrecy

Even from second story windows, kids can be very clever about sneaking out of the house without parents detecting it. Once you finally get past your own denial, you must play detective. Look for:

1. A decline in school grades
2. Absenteeism from school
3. Temper outbursts
4. Long periods of isolation in which your teen has

sequestered himself within his bedroom, or simply stays away from home.

Ask him if you can meet his friends. Chances are, if he's abusing drugs, he won't introduce you to them because they will tend to give him away by their behavior and appearance (although looks can be deceiving). Also, one of them will be affectionately known as "Snake." Don't bother even asking to meet "Snake"; he will be stricken from your list of allowable friends on the basis of his nickname alone.

Another suggestion: Not only get to know your teen's friends, but his friend's parents as well (except for Mr. and Mrs. Snake). Parents have been known to have some useful information from time to time. And getting a feel for how motivated the other set of parents are to supervise their own kids can't hurt.

●Availability

Drugs are a prevalent fact of life in our society. If your teen wants something badly enough, he can get it. It's one thing for him to sit in his classroom or your living room and agree with the latest "just say no" campaign. It's quite another when he's "cruising" with the guys and someone pulls out a joint. Allowing your teen to associate with kids who are already using drugs or alcohol is setting him up. That's why the family contract addresses this issue as a "Most Important Rule."

●The Depression Decoy

It's true. Drug or alcohol abuse can lead to depression—which provides even less motivation to get into a treatment program. But depression can also be a ploy to avoid treatment altogether.

Listen to this scenario: An addict states he has become aware that he's "really" depressed; he realizes now that he was drinking or taking drugs to "treat" his depression. He describes the drug abuse as "secondary" to his "primary" disorder—which is depression. So ... any dis-

cussion of sobriety would just be a "Band-Aid" approach
to the problem. As he tells his therapist, "Let's not waste
our valuable time talking about drugs and alcohol, doctor. Let's talk about the *real* problem." (Which is, once
again, depression.) This convoluted logic might sound
smart, but it's still a rationalization to avoid dealing
directly with the drug or drinking problem.

While it is certainly true that depression and substance abuse usually do go hand in hand, saying that
the depression is causing the abuse is an oversimplifica-
tion. In fact, effective treatment for depression necessi-
tates sobriety:

1. The depression itself often lifts without the influence of drugs or alcohol.
2. An assessment of the patient will be skewed by the
   personality or mood changes brought on by the drug.
3. Psychotherapy cannot be conducted in any mean-
   ingful way when addiction, with its resulting memory impairment and decreased concentration, is
   present.
4. Antidepressants can't be taken with drugs or alcohol. The combination can be dangerous.

AFTER DENIAL, WHAT?

Once parents recognize that their child is indeed using
drugs or alcohol, what do they do? Panic is the most
popular choice. Secret plans are made to move to another city to get away from the "problem troublemaker
kids" in the area. However, upon reviewing the current
prevalence of substance abuse among American youth, I
have discovered only two remaining towns that do not
have an adolescent drug problem in their communities.
For some reason, they both have "Gulch" in their names.

Other parents nix the "get out of town" idea in favor of
the "let's play Detective Kojak" approach. Here, parents
take what I consider useful advice to an extreme. Don-
ning traditional trenchcoats, shaving their heads, and

developing a real nasty habit of sucking on Tootsie Pops,
they plant bugging devices on the Snoopy phone they
bought their child last week. After five minutes of
wiretapping, they have enough evidence on their kid to
link him not only with drugs, but with both Kennedy
assassinations as well....

Another parental response is one I nicknamed the
"let's call every one of my kid's friends, their parents,
grandparents, and favorite pet to let them know they all
better stay away from my kid or I'm calling the cops
next time" technique. In the process of running the
phone bill into five figures, these parents also manage to
discuss the drug problem with everyone but their child.

In humor, there is truth and, if they haven't actually
carried through with the above suggestions, many parents have at least given them real thought.

But if these time-honored approaches won't work, what
will? In two words:

SUPPORT GROUPS

There's nothing like experience when it comes to dealing with kids. In fact, lots and lots of advice from people
who have already been through it with their kids is
pretty much a necessity to stop substance abuse—and
prevent it from coming back.

Parent support groups fit the bill perfectly. Here, parents actually band together for the main purpose of
exchanging experience and ideas on raising kids with
substance abuse problems. Parents generously offer new
members the wisdom they learned from their mistakes
(and their Aunt Angelina's recipe for canelloni). With
the shroud of family shame and embarrassment cast
aside once and for all, a free and open discussion of the
hardcore issues surrounding drug abuse is finally possible—
and so is help and hope.

These parent support groups are usually affiliated
with larger nonprofit community groups, such as Alcoholics
Anonymous, Narcotics Anonymous, Cocaine Anonymous,

Alateen, Al-anon, and the Palmer Drug Abuse Program. These larger organizations share a common goal for their members: total abstinence from all forms of drugs and alcohol. They advise their members to get rid of all drug paraphenalia; they provide social interaction, such as mixers and dances, that have nothing to do with alcohol or drugs.

These groups have had remarkable success—and they've taught mental health professionals many valuable lessons. AA, for example, reaches an estimated 650,000 American adolescents and adults afflicted with alcoholism; it has become an integral part of most modern hospital-based and outpatient treatment programs.

MINIMIZING THE RISKS

No, we can't singlehandedly get rid of this national epidemic. But we can circumvent substance abuse problems within our own homes with the family contract. Here's how:

*Meet their friends. As I'd mentioned earlier, not hanging around with kids who do drugs or alcohol is a crucial "Most Important Rule." If your kid insists that their friends are "unavailable," "too shy," or "not into meeting parents," firmly tell her that that is unfortunate since she won't be allowed to associate with those people until they somehow show up at your door.

*Implement a urine drug test. Many parents find the thought of conducting drug tests on their own children repugnant. It is an unpleasant reminder of impaired trust between parent and child, but some kids are actually quite receptive to the idea; they feel it provides an extra push to stay sober. Its inclusion within the family contract should not be explained as an example of dishonesty between parent and child. Instead, it should be looked at as a statement of mistrust—but only in the sense that your child cannot yet trust his own impulse control. This way it's seen as a positive step, one that, if administered properly, can be seen as a cooperative effort by the entire family.

*Supervise your teen's money. If your child keeps "losing" her allowance or offers vague and inadequate explanations as to how it all got spent, get suspicious. And, above all, don't give her any more money; enforcing the allowance privilege is critical right now. (Similarly, if one day you notice that your kid's wearing a Rolex, it's time for a talk.)

*Watch your child's activity and social level. Watch your teen's grades at school. If he goes from being a B student who runs track and goes out with several different friends pretty much every weekend to a failing student who spends virtually all his time in his room listening to Ratt, there's a problem going on. But thanks to the family contract, however, none of this will come as a surprise. You'll have seen him go from a Level Four to a Level One—with all the "grounding" that implies. You'll have kept on top of the situation—and be ready to seek professional help, if necessary.

*Clothes and dress can be deceiving. There are kids out there with chicken bones connecting their nose and right ear who are totally drug- and alcohol-free. There are also kids in complete Ralph Lauren cowboy outfits who experience visual hallucinations of an entire shopping mall after doing "a few hits" of "Ecstasy." Just because your teen is dressing in black these days doesn't mean a thing—especially if she's completing all her chores and rules on time and in synch.

*Physical health is a more reliable indicator of possible drug abuse. Recurrent sore throats, sinus infections, coughing spells, vomiting, bellyaches, weight loss, sleep disturbances, and low energy are all possible signs of drug or alcohol abuse. Look at the "Exercise" and "Routine Chores" Rules. A reduction in the usual level of physical activity can be significant.

Treating substance abuse is a combination of psychotherapy, behavior modification, group support, medication, and family communication. It can't be done alone and, if you suspect your teen is in trouble, you must seek out professional help.

Closing Remarks: The Author As Guinea Pig

When I introduced the family contract into our home, it was not without some sense of desperation. My wife and I were getting hoarse from repeating the parents' chant:

Clean your room, wash your hands, go to bed
Clean your room, wash your hands, go to bed
Clean your...

In the meantime, the rooms stayed messy, hands were dirty, and the kids were up all night while we had resorted to simply blockading the kids from our bedroom. (We cleverly made creative use of several extra patio bricks.) When I introduced the concept of the contract to my wife during one particular patio brick blockade, she felt it was worth a try. We presented it to the kids—and, as you now know from reading this book, it was initially received with a certain amount of protest. But, as you also know, the contract had a great deal of success from Day One.

Now, several months ago, my older daughter requested a rather unusual birthday present. She wanted to be taken off the level system for a week. After some thought my wife and I decided, "why not?" Lauren had been on Level Four for many weeks. And, after all, we all take vacations from work—why not from the contract? (Frankly, it would be a vacation for us, too. There are some days when sitting down and totaling up points after work is not first and foremost on your mind.)

Well, the contract still worked in the sense that a train still goes down the tracks for several miles after you shut off the engine. By the end of that one week, my wife and I saw a slight deterioration in the quality of my daughter's chores and in her overall behavior. She also began to get a little whiny. She must have told me over fifty time in two days that she wanted to stop the "stupid" family contract altogether....

But, interestingly, when the family contract was reinstated, the whining stopped.

I was not surprised; after all, the family contract has been proven to work in modern psychiatric facilities. In fact, it is a part of Laurelwood Hospital's—and many other successful hospitals'—standard therapeutic techniques. This book represents an effort to bring this family contract into the home *before* things get to a point where hospitalization becomes necessary. Hopefully, it can become a form of preventive medicine.

So...does it work? An emphatic yes. But, like anything else, it must be tended. It must be watched, nourished, and adapted to the viscissitudes of life.

Before I end this book, I leave you with this thought: "You can lead a horse to water, but you can't make him drink" is a mistake. The philosophy of the family contract says "go ahead and lead the horse to water"—knowing that we might not be able to make him drink, but knowing that when he gets thirsty enough, he'll probably drink.

In fact, he'll be thankful he's already at that watering hole.

Here's to your horse—and your watering hole.

FAMILY CONTRACT
for

The Most Important Rules
Breaking these rules means going to Level One for at least a week.

No physical violence (hitting, kicking, biting, throwing things, damaging property)

No running away from home or sneaking out

No taking drugs or alcohol

No playing with kids who use drugs and alcohol

No lying to parents

No sexual acting out

Always must do what Mom and Dad say

FAMILY CONTRACT for _____
Week of _____

RULE/(POINTS)	Sun	M	T	W	Th	F	Sat
Routine Chores (such as pet care, clean room, lawn care) (0-3)							
Special Chores (such as wash car, laundry, ironing, repairs, clean garage) (0-3)							
In Bed By Bedtime/ Curfew (0-2)							
School Behavior (0-2) On Time (0-1) Homework (0-5)							
Art - draw picture, write story or poetry (0-2)							
Lessons - tutoring, music, dance, sports or art (0-3)							
Practice - music, sports, dance or art (0-3)							
Other exercise (0-3)							
Read - book or newspaper (not from school) (0-3)							
Religious - attend church, Sunday school, etc. (0-3)							
Personal hygiene and appearance (0-3)							
Medical Therapy (0-3)							
General attitude and behavior (0-3)							
Daily Total							

Weekly Point Total _____ = **Level** _____

LEVEL PRIVILEGES
For ages 5 to 10

PRIVILEGE	LEVEL			
	(by weekly point totals)			
	I	II	III	IV
	(0-30)	(31-60)	(61-90)	(over 90)
Allowance (per week)	0	$1	$2	$3
Phone (minutes per day)	0	10	30	60
Special privilege (such as overnite guests, movies, prize or gift)	no	no	1/week	2/week
Television	none	1 hr/day	1 hr/day on school days 2 hrs/day on weekends	1 hr/day on school days unlimited on weekends
Outside play	none	1 hr/day 3 hrs/day on wknds	2 hr/day on school days 6 hrs/day on weekends	4 hrs/day on school days unlimited on weekends
Bedtime	8 PM	8:15 PM	8:30 PM on school nites 11 PM on weekends	9 PM on school nites 11 PM on weekends

I, _____,
have read the Family Contract, understand it, and am willing to try to
follow it. I understand that in signing this contract, I might disagree
with part of it or all of it, but I will follow the rules in it just the same.

_____   _____   _____
(son or daughter)   Dad   Mom
                               (witness)   (witness)

LEVEL PRIVILEGES

For ages 10 to 15

PRIVILEGE	LEVEL			
	(by weekly point totals)			
	I	II	III	IV
	(0-30)	(31-60)	(61-90)	(over 90)
Allowance (per week)	0	$1	$2	$5
Phone (minutes per day)	0	10	30	60
Special privilege (such as overnite guests, movies, prize or gift)	no	no	1/week	2/week
Television	none	1 hr/day	1 hr/day on school days 2 hrs/day on weekends	1 hr/day on school days unlimited on weekends
Outside play	none	1 hr/day 3 hrs/day on wknds weekends	2 hr/day on school days 4 hrs/day on weekends	2 hrs/day on school days 6 hrs/day on
Bedtime	8 PM	8:30 PM	9 PM on school nites 11 PM on weekends	10 PM on school nites 1 AM on weekends
Unsupervised time	none	none	none on school days 4 hrs/day on weekends	2hr/day on school days 6 hrs/day on weekends
Curfew	no outside play	6 PM	8 PM on school nites 10 PM on weekends	9 PM on school nites 11 PM on weekends

I, _____,
have read the Family Contract, understand it, and am willing to try to
follow it. I understand that in signing this contract, I might disagree
with part of it or all of it, but I will follow the rules in it just the same.

_____	_____	_____
(son or daughter)	Dad (witness)	Mom (witness)

LEVEL PRIVILEGES

For ages 16 to 18

PRIVILEGE	LEVEL			
	(by weekly point totals)			
	I	II	III	IV
	(0-30)	(31-60)	(61-90)	(over 90)
Allowance (per week)	0	$2	$5	$10
Phone (minutes per day)	0	10	30	60
Special privilege (such as overnite guests, movies, prize or gift)	no	no	1/week	2/week
Television	none	1 hr/day	1 hr/day on school days 2 hrs/day on weekends	1 hr/day on school days unlimited on weekends
Outside play	none	1 hr/day 3 hrs/day on wknds	2 hr/day on school days 6 hrs/day on weekends	4 hrs/day on school days 12 hrs on weekends
Bedtime	8 PM	8:30 PM	9:30 PM on school nites 11 PM on weekends	10:30 PM on school nites 1 AM on weekends
Unsupervised time	none	none	2hr/day on school days 6 hrs/day on weekends	4hr/day on school days 12 hrs/day on weekends
Curfew	no outside activities	6 PM	8:30 PM on school nites 10 PM on weekends	9:30 PM on school nites 1 AM on weekends
Car privileges (when age appropriate)	no	no	2 hrs/week	6 hrs/week

I, _____,
have read the Family Contract, understand it, and am willing to try to follow it. I understand that in signing this contract, I might disagree with part of it or all of it, but I will follow the rules in it just the same.

_____   _____   _____
(son or daughter)   Dad   Mom
                                        (witness)   (witness)